BRIAN DOWLING &
ARTHUR GOUROUNLIAN'S

MODERN
FAMILY

BRIAN DOWLING GOUROUNLIAN AND ARTHUR GOUROUNLIAN are among Ireland's most beloved television personalities and social media stars. The internet exploded when the couple announced they were expecting their first child, with Brian's sister Aoife acting as their surrogate.

BRIAN rose to fame after winning the second season of reality series *Big Brother* in 2001 and went on to win *Ultimate Big Brother* in 2010. He then went on to host *Big Brother* after Davina McCall in 2011, when the hugely popular show moved to Channel 5. Brian has also worked with other channels, including ITV1, ITV2, and ITVBe in the UK and is a regular face on Virgin Media in Ireland. Brian's podcast about grief, *Death Becomes Him*, has two million downloads, and he currently presents 98FM's mid-morning show with Suzanne Kane.

ARTHUR is a professional dancer, choreographer and creative director who has worked with some of the world's biggest music stars, including Beyoncé, Kylie Minogue and One Direction. He is a judge on RTÉ's *Dancing with* *the Stars* and was also a judge representing Armenia on the American show *The World's Best* hosted by James Corden. Arthur is also credited with getting renowned designer Christian Louboutin to dance in his own shoes when he launched his first line of men's footwear.

Together **BRIAN AND ARTHUR** have over 843,000 social media followers. They live in County Kildare with their daughter Blake. Brian and Arthur's journey to parenthood was also the subject of a successful TV documentary programme, produced by Kite Entertainment and broadcast on RTÉ television in spring 2023.

BRIAN DOWLING &
ARTHUR GOUROUNLIAN'S

MODERN
FAMILY

BIRTHS, MARRIAGES, DEATHS
AND EVERYTHING IN BETWEEN

GILL BOOKS

Gill Books
Hume Avenue
Park West
Dublin 12
www.gillbooks.ie

Gill Books is an imprint of M.H. Gill and Co.

9780717198481

Edited by Meg Walker
Copyedited by Susan McKeever
Printed and bound in Great Britain by Clays Ltd, Elcograf S.p.A.
This book is typeset in Minion Pro.

*The paper used in this book comes from the wood pulp of
sustainably managed forests.*

A CIP catalogue record for this book is available from the
British Library.

5 4 3 2 1

To our daughter Blake, who amazes us all every day;
our wonderful surrogate, Aoife; our exceptionally
supportive and loving parents and family members;
and to modern families everywhere.

CONTENTS

Introduction xi

PART ONE

1 Brian: Rathangan, County Kildare, Ireland 3
2 Arthur: Armenia and Belgium 21
3 Brian: London 55
4 Arthur: From Europe to the UK 87

PART TWO

5 Brian and Arthur: Beginning our new
   life together 119
6 Brian and Rosie 133
7 Brian and Arthur: From LA to Ireland 163
8 Brian, Arthur and Aoife: Straffan,
   County Kildare, Ireland 183
9 Brian and Blake 203
10 Arthur and Blake 233

Acknowledgements 251

INTRODUCTION

Writing this book, the two of us have explored our individual pasts as well as our life together and let us just say, it has been an emotional rollercoaster. Looking back on the night we first met – two young gay men in their twenties living in London and having the craic – we never could have imagined we'd now be living in Ireland and raising our amazing daughter together.

But all of that didn't come without a fight – a fight to discover who we are as individuals; who we could become as partners; the struggle to be taken seriously in our careers; the rigmarole we'd have to go through just to get married and to later have the child we so desperately wanted. We even had to fight at times for survival.

This is a story about love in all its many magical forms and the pain that life can sometimes bring. We hope in sharing our memories – both happy and sad – and retelling the tales of our youth as two individuals as well as a couple, that the readers of this book will find inspiration to take into their own lives.

This is a story about how our family came to be. Life is a crazy journey of twists and turns and sliding doors. It's sometimes really hard and at other times extraordinarily joyful. And sometimes you don't want to get out of bed but you just keep going. No one knows what's around the corner or what other people are going through beneath the surface.

We have one wish for all the readers of this book: that you realise that anything is possible with hard work and determination, that you are worthy. Don't let anyone stop you from living the life you want. Surround yourself with the best people that make you feel like a superstar – and you do the same for them. And never give up – neither of us gave up on anything we truly wanted, including each other.

That said, without the love and support of our family and friends, without the sacrifices made by our incredible parents, we both know we never would have made it to this point. We're extremely grateful for every single moment of the past four-plus decades, as each one took us to where we are today – our happily ever after.

BRIAN AND ARTHUR

PART ONE

1

BRIAN:

Rathangan, County Kildare, Ireland

One of the defining facts of my life is that I was born into a very large family in rural Ireland. The only boy in a household of nine unique individuals, each with their own incredible personality, I was fortunate to experience a childhood that was filled with love and support. The close bond I had with my parents and six sisters has informed my values and kept me grounded through the ups and downs of my life, giving me a sense of safety and security I could always fall back on.

I came screaming into the world on 13 June 1978, the eldest of seven children. The next month, my mum, Rosie, was pregnant with my sister Michelle. She was born in April, so there were just ten months between us. We were in the same class at school, we made our Communion together, our Confirmation together, started secondary school together and sat the Junior Cert together. Then Michelle did Transition Year and I went straight to Fifth Year. At school, we pretended we were twins because we were so embarrassed that we were so close in age.

One time, when we were older, Michelle and I examined an ashtray our mum and dad got as a wedding gift. It said, '1 April 1978'. That's when we realised something was up. If they got married in April '78 and I was born in June '78, that would mean Mum was with child when she got married! We were in such shock. When we put it to Mum, she just said, 'Oh, they just put the wrong date on it. It should have been April 1977'. She had a habit of fudging stuff like that. But, funnily enough, if Mum saw a woman with a young baby who was pregnant again, she'd say she 'got caught'.

My sister Valerie arrived in 1980, and then Tracey, Paula, Aoife and our youngest sister, Tara, followed. So, I was the only boy among six sisters. Growing up, I suppose I was spoiled because I was Mum's only son. I had my own bedroom while the girls had to share, I wore brand-new clothes while the girls were subjected to an endless recycling of hand-me-downs. Even when it came to chores, Mum would say, 'You girls do the washing up and let Brian study.'

We were always the last to get the memo on Mum's pregnancies. Every time a new baby arrived, we honestly didn't even know she was pregnant. She was very good at hiding it and would only start to show towards the end. Tara was born in November, and I remember Mum only telling us a month before. She also never told anyone her due date.

'When are you due?'

'Soon,' she'd reply.

She didn't purposely hide her pregnancies, she just never told anyone.

I once noted to my mum that when she had Tara, she was only 35. That was probably considered old back then, but I asked her why she and our dad, Gerry, didn't have any more children. She just said, 'We were never blessed again.' And I thought, what an incredible thing to say. To put her body through the trauma of having seven children and count each one of us a blessing. Mum was selfless. Her priorities were her children and her husband. And we were all her best friends. She didn't really have a social life, everything was about her children. Our dad worked in construction and would go to work early and get home late. We'd see him at the weekends while Mum ran the home all week.

Our mother was traditional, but also very open-minded. She never judged anyone and always encouraged us to be nice, kind, respectful and to show the family off in the best possible way. She would say, 'When you leave this house, you stand united as a family. If you kids want to fight and call each other names, do all that at home behind closed doors.' Mum would always say to us that the guards had never come to her door. It might sound like a low bar but it was something she was so proud of.

I had what one might call a very 'normal' upbringing in Rathangan. When we were kids, we'd walk two, three, four fields away from our house. We'd bring sandwiches and go berry-picking. We'd cross rivers to go to the next field, even though none of us could swim. But there was never any sense of danger; we never thought anything bad could happen. We used to play tennis on the road outside our house during the summers and had one cousin watching one way for a car while another was keeping an eye on the other direction. You couldn't do any of that now – four or five kids, with no adults, between the ages of maybe five and eleven going on day trips or picnics together.

We played rounders or swapped fancy paper. Looking back on it, I miss that time, and now I see my nieces and nephews and they're talking about TikTok dances and Instagram and watching stuff on screens. When I tell them that we would play Snakes and Ladders, they'd be like, 'Why would you play that?'

We didn't have a landline in the house. We'd go across the road to our neighbour, Mrs Mullally, with 20p or 50p to make phone calls. We had a small car and it would hold nine people, with Mum and Dad in the front, one child on Mum's knee, four children in the back and two in the boot. My father raised greyhounds, so we'd smell of dogs and be covered in their hair. I don't think anyone wore seatbelts. It really was a different time.

We were very working class. There was no spare money – we never went on holidays, never had a nice car, but we had plenty of food, warmth, clothing, school-books, uniforms ... I don't know how my parents actually did it, but every Christmas, when it came to Santa, we would have so much waiting for us by the tree. My mum *loved* Christmas. I think that's why I'm obsessed with Christmas to this day. She enjoyed holiday traditions year round – on Valentine's Day, we'd get Valentine's cards and I swear they were in different handwriting, and yet they were all from Mum. We'd still have Easter eggs in the summer. That's not a joke. And we'd still have Christmas food at Easter – my mum would buy these hampers where you'd pay two pounds a week throughout the year. I remember the boxes of Scots Clan, along with Tayto, red lemonade, white lemonade and cream soda. And I remember the excitement when Chocolate Kimberleys first came out.

We were never allowed in the sitting room unless it was Christmas, so by the time December rolled around and we'd finally get a chance to go into the sitting room, it was such a treat. There was a three-seater sofa, two armchairs and an open fire. That felt opulent. I felt like we were rich for those moments. The television would be in the corner, and then over the television you'd have the glasses in the cabinet, and under that you'd have the plates and all the festive goodies. The wood would be crackling in the fire and I'd be snug on the couch. It felt so cosy. Going to the bog to bring home turf for the fire … for us, that was like going on a holiday. Mum would pack sandwiches in tin foil, crisps, treats and big flasks of tea, and we'd all go down to the bog. And then we'd fight to be the kid that would sit on top of the turf on the trailer for the two-mile drive back home. It's ludicrous when you think about it now. At the bog, we would be rolling up the peat and throwing it at each other. There'd be horseflies and Mum would have a hat and a picnic blanket. To us, it was a day out.

It was a very typical rural Irish upbringing. We grew up in the country, near farms. We walked and cycled everywhere. There was no other option because my dad worked all day and Mum couldn't drive. Dad was gone from six or seven in the morning, so when we got up for school, we would cycle. When there was snow or frost, we were on those bicycles. We were slipping, we were falling. Whether there'd be floods or rain, or thunder and lightning, it made no difference. That was the only way we could get to school. And now my nieces and nephews don't cycle anywhere. They're driven, or maybe some of them are old enough to walk some of the way. But back then, everyone cycled and we'd call into each other's houses and all cycle together, three, four abreast.

In secondary school we'd study late, so we wouldn't get home until six o'clock and we'd cycle in the dark. I remember my parents got me a second-hand racer bike and we spray-painted it silver. The brakes were so bad, I'd have to put my foot down coming down the hill and it would wear the leather of the right-hand side of my shoe and Mum would patch it up. Sometimes she'd put tyre patches on my shoe because she couldn't afford to get me brand-new shoes that I liked.

I was so lucky growing up. Sometimes I feel guilty when I say we didn't have money, but I don't think we actually needed it. While Dad worked in construction and held numerous jobs, there was a time when he was out of work. There was little money in Ireland back then and few building sites, and I remember us all being quite scared for our dad at that point. But my sisters and I always rallied around our parents.

Mum always encouraged us to get jobs as soon as we could. I got my first job at 12 years old, working in a dog kennel for friends of my parents, walking dogs and cleaning up after them. We were allowed to keep the money for ourselves, so when it came to Third Year, when it was time to buy exam papers, I did all of that myself. I bought a brand new mountain bike to replace the second-hand one I had before. I'd buy my own uniform and have nice things. Our parents instilled that in us. If you wanted something, you'd have to work for it. I've learned that no one is going to give you anything in this world – you've got to get it yourself. You've got to work for it. And all my sisters have that, too. I knew the more I worked, the more money I'd get and I could buy what I wanted with it. When you're a kid, you don't worry about budgeting – you're not paying rent, you're not paying bills. But then as I got older, and still lived at home, I'd give Mum maybe 20 pounds a week from my wages. It felt nice to be able to do that.

When I was doing my Junior Cert, I got a job in a chipper in Rathangan and would finish on a Saturday at 4 a.m. and cycle home a mile and a half in the dark. No reflectors, no light. I'd get up later that morning and go in to do the day shift, come home, go back and do the night shift, finish 'early' on a Sunday at 2 a.m., cycle home again, get up and go to school on Monday. Christmas Day, we'd go to the dog kennel and walk the dogs, have breakfast there, come home for the day, go back in the evening, and then do all that again on Stephen's Day because we'd get double the pay for working the holidays.

I loved working in the takeaway. It was so much fun because I'm such a gossip that I'd chat with everyone. When the festivals were on, I'd be so busy. I hadn't a clue what a full Irish was. I was cracking eggs on the hot plate, bacon and sausages in the fryer. The club would be open, with people coming in and ordering food afterwards. I didn't drink back then – never drank, never smoked; on nights out, I'd drink Fanta or Lucozade, so it was weird for me to see people drunk.

Michelle and I were so close but we were also each other's nemesis. We'd be physically fighting – pushing each other, pulling each other's hair, and my sisters would stand around chanting one or the other's names. When we think back at that now, we laugh. We had so much fun. Mum loved television and got me into the big soap dramas like *Falcon Crest, The Colbys, Knots Landing, Dynasty* …

Alexis and Krystle would have these cat fights. I was into all of that, which is probably why I'm so dramatic now.

One thing my mum was very good at was encouraging me to iron my own clothes, to look after myself, to know how to cook. Again, there's that unique mix of her being somewhat old-fashioned and yet very modern and practical in her values. When I did home economics in school, my mother was very supportive. Not many boys did that class – I think it was just me and one other guy.

*****

I remember one time in primary school when I was around ten or eleven years old, there was a teacher in my school who hit me because I was laughing. He whacked me across the face. I knew my mother and father would have wanted me to stand up and tell him not to do that to me, and I remember pushing my chair back to get up, but something stopped me. I never told my parents that happened and then a few weeks later, one Saturday, they found out. I'd never before seen my mother change the way she did that day – the veins in her neck, she was red and pacing. She was furious. In her mind, I was completely violated and abused by this teacher. That Monday morning, I was in school and suddenly I saw out of the corner of my eye my dad's old blue car driving into the car park. My parents came straight into the building and knocked on the door of my classroom. The teacher went out to meet them and they absolutely lifted him out of it. My father, who was once a boxer, politely said, 'If you ever put your hands on my son again, I'll do the exact same to you.' The teacher was shook when he came back in. I don't think anyone had ever held him accountable before.

*****

I suppose I've always known I was gay, in a weird way. There was never any 'coming out'. It was very matter-of-fact. I went to a mixed school until I made my Communion and then I went to a Catholic boys' school until Sixth Class. There were times I'd go to Mass twice a day – during Lent, we'd go as a family every day and then we'd go again during school. I had faith. And I always had friends, always had a laugh, and would be invited to parties. I did the community games and played football. Nothing ever really clicked when I was in primary school. At age 12 and 13, I knew girls liked me. It was probably when I was in secondary school that I started having those feelings. I remember thinking in Third Year, *I'm not really into girls.* And I'd see some guy and think, *I like him.* It wasn't really until Sixth Year that I realised I was definitely gay – I wasn't attracted to girls at all.

I don't recall ever being bullied or beaten up for being gay while growing up. I do remember words being used – like pansy, sissy, queer – but it was never to a point where I ever felt threatened. I always felt safe. And I was very quick-witted – being funny helps when you're different. Then secondary school was a little different, because you're dealing with new people and students who are much older than you, but I still never felt threatened at school. Looking back now, the guys who would have called me queer, gay, pansy … I wish I'd had the confidence then to say, 'What's your point?' But this was 1989, 1990. I didn't know what being gay was – I had no idea what it meant. There was no representation for me on television. I was very limited. And I was living in the countryside.

During Sixth Year, I went to my career guidance teacher and told him I wanted to be an air steward. He roared at me, 'Do not say this outside of these four walls. People will laugh at you. Just work in a hotel, don't do that job.' I remember feeling really embarrassed and I went home to tell my mum. She said to me, 'No, if you want to do that job, you absolutely should.' Mum and Dad paid for me to go to an intense airline training academy in Waterford run by Frances Roche – it was about £300 or £400 Irish punts. We got headshots taken and they drove me down to Waterford. That was in 1996 or 1997, and I got a job in Ryanair in 1998. Mum was so proud. I find it very odd that my career guidance teacher was horrified that I wanted to be a flight attendant. He probably thought it wasn't a job for a man. I wanted to be cabin crew, and I wanted to escape. I wanted to explore my sexuality. I kind of knew, living in Rathangan, that I was never going to meet other gay people there. You naively feel you're the only person going through it. It feels so singular.

Around 1997, when I was 19 and still living at home, working the tills in Dunnes Stores, I went on a holiday to Spain with two friends. We were on the beach and they'd left to get some shade and I stayed. Then I spotted this guy looking over at me and thought, *that's odd – what's he looking at?* He suddenly emptied a bottle of water and put a piece of paper inside the bottle, closed the lid, placed the bottle in the sand and walked off. I walked over, picked it up and ran back to my towel to open it. The note read: *I think you're really cute. If you fancied going for dinner, here is my number.* I remember thinking, what does this mean? I went and told the girls I was on holidays with. We'd never had a conversation before about me being gay, and they were like, 'Oh my God, you have to go for it.' There was no judgement. So I contacted him and we went for dinner. He was a holiday rep. He paid. It was so odd. I was so young, a virgin at that point, very naive about everything, but I was also curious. We started to make out and fooled around and I remember just feeling really dirty afterwards. I was thinking, *oh my God, what have I done?* There was such guilt, such shame. However, it was all inner shame. It wasn't coming from anyone else. I went back to where the girls were staying and was just inconsolable. They were like, 'What happened?' I said, 'Nothing, I wasn't assaulted or anything.'

The next day, I walked down to the beach and kept walking into the water. I can't swim. The water was up past my waist. I just felt so dirty. I felt vulnerable. I felt like I had disappointed myself. I felt shame at a level I'd never felt before. It was a horrible feeling. The water was quite calm and it was above my belly button. And I suddenly just had this sense of clarity, a voice inside me saying, *what are you doing? Just get out of the water.*

I'm grateful my survival instincts kicked in that day but clearly, despite the incredible support I received my whole life from my family and those friends I was with, it wasn't enough to counteract the impact of growing up in a society where LGBTQ+ people were hidden from view, where being gay was considered a 'sin'. That shame I felt while standing in the water was coming from a place deep down inside me that developed through life in a country where homosexuality was only decriminalised in 1993, when I had just turned 15. It would take some time before I could feel comfortable being my true self.

I'm very lucky that my struggle with my sexuality was an inner one. I can't imagine what would have happened to me if that was coming from family members or friends.

Would I have kept walking into the sea? The girls who were there with me in Spain were full of love and compassion for me – the only person judging me was me. And that was a hard thing to grapple with. And because my first experience with another man was so negative, I think that became the kind of relationship I got myself into in the beginning – with men who weren't good for me. Thankfully, I eventually grew out of that phase, and met the man of my dreams. When I think about my early years, overall they were remarkably blessed, given what my future husband was going through in Armenia.

2

ARTHUR:

Armenia and Belgium

My childhood in Armenia is a blur. There are memories I can recall vaguely, like flashes, but I don't remember happiness. My parents did their best to create happiness for me and my sister, Nazik, but from 1987 to 1992, those were catastrophic years.

My earliest memory is from when I was seven years old. I was born on 1 June 1980 and in 1987, we moved to a new home. It was a three-bedroom apartment on the tenth floor. We were one of the first families to move into this territory. My mum, Maria, was the one who got that apartment for us – she was working for a food company for ten years and through a special employment law at that time, she was presented with this apartment by the government. We were very lucky. The area was neglected and a lot of people living there were poor. My family were middle class – not poor or rich, but okay. My dad, Hakob, was doing everything he could to support us, working in a factory with his father. The local schoolchildren wore these red scarves, and I was so excited to start school, which I did shortly after we moved there. Meanwhile, my mum started teaching Russian in a local school because she wanted to work near our new home, and I started learning the Russian language. We lived in this area for about a year before a 6.8 magnitude earthquake hit in December 1988.

It was the biggest earthquake Armenia had ever seen. I will never forget that day: that was the first time I nearly died. I was the oldest and tallest in my class and was always sitting in the back of the classroom. I got up from my chair and when I started walking, I bounced left and right. We didn't know what was happening. The cabinets of the library at the back of the room then fell on my desk. It was like a horror movie. The whole building then just went. We started jumping out of windows. I survived, and we were okay, but our school was destroyed. I went home, and when I got there, I learned we were not allowed in our building. For about two weeks, everybody had to camp outside. After the earthquake, everything was destroyed and people struggled to recover. We weren't really living during that time – we were just surviving.

Then in 1990, Armenia decided to separate from the USSR. I remember the referendum so clearly – there were posters everywhere saying, 'Yes or No: Vote Yes to leave or No to stay'. And I thought, *why would you leave Russia? They're providing our food and everything.* I was ten at the time, wondering, *if we leave, how will we eat?* As soon as Armenia separated from Russia, the next day the food store shelves were all empty. Overnight, the Russians came and cleaned out Armenia. For two years, we didn't have electricity or gas. We'd go outside and cut down trees and gather wood to heat our homes. By that time, all four of us were sharing one bedroom. We were given electricity for one hour for the whole family. We'd have coupons; if you were a family of four, you were only allowed 250g of bread per week. I remember queuing for that. Because there was no food, kids in my school were collapsing in front of our eyes from starvation. It just became the norm because there was nothing we could do. And because there was no electricity, we had to study by candlelight.

Then in 1992, war broke out with Azerbaijan and things got worse again. Everything was dark for me. One day, my grandmother, who adored me, was visiting and asked my mum if I could come and stay at her house. I felt poorly so Mum suggested I stay with my grandmother the following week instead. My grandma returned home and the next morning she went to visit a neighbour's house for coffee. In the courtyard, where people were living and children were playing, there was a garage and a guy was selling guns and bombs to the Armenian troops. That garage exploded suddenly and the whole building collapsed. Lots of people died that day, including my grandmother. Ironically enough, had she stayed in her own apartment, she might have survived, as her side of the building was still intact after the explosion, but her friend's home was completely gone. I was devastated to lose my beloved grandmother but also shocked because I was meant to be there. I felt like I had been saved, yet again, for some reason.

Looking back on my childhood, there aren't many good memories from that time, but I always wanted to be artistic, and loved to dance. When I was ten, there was a popular dance troupe that performed on TV and my aunt knew someone who could get me an audition. They thought I was talented and invited me to join. I was the youngest boy dancing there. It was a small spark of joy while everything was collapsing around us and I clung to it.

In 1991, I went to a music school established by Charles Aznavour, the famous Armenian-French singer, to provide talented people with an opportunity to study music. I was 11 years old, had a good ear for music, and did the entry exam. A teacher there approached my mum and said she wanted me in her class. My mum asked what class she taught, and it was violin. Mum said to her, 'I know my son – he would never do violin. He has no patience for it. He likes drums or guitar.' The teacher pleaded with her so she said, 'okay, give it a try.' I hated it because I'm so energetic and the violin was too boring for me. I just loved loudness.

Then one day when I was 13, I was coming out of music school and went back inside to get something, so my friends went ahead of me. A van pulled up. They were looking for tall boys to fight in the war with Azerbaijan. I saw one of my friends taken by the arms and shoved into the van. My other friend managed to run away. When I went home that day, I told my parents what happened. My mum was shaking. That was when the panic started. My parents said, 'That's it. We need to leave this country.' My mum's sister was working in a public service type of job in Yerevan, the capital of Armenia, and had a lot of connections. She arranged to get us a holiday visa. You couldn't just leave the country – everything was closed. So, we had to pretend we were just going on a holiday.

*****

That was my childhood. There's nothing of beauty there. I vaguely recall little things here and there. When I see pictures now – there are only a handful of them – I don't recognise anything. I've probably blocked out all those memories. It's like somebody took a chip that stored all memories from before 1987 out of my head. I only see darkness when I think of Armenia.

It took about a month to get the visa, which was for Denmark. I didn't know where Denmark was or how we would get there. I knew nothing about Europe. The only place you'd know about in Armenia is Paris – the Eiffel

Tower – or Los Angeles, because that's where so many Armenians would go. My dad started taking stuff from the factory to sell so we'd have money before we left. We packed one bag each and our long journey began by bus. It was so difficult – the doors couldn't close because the bus was so full of people trying to get out of the country. My parents were mapping the journey and we were to go through Russia.

There was one frightening incident on our journey that I will never forget. We were on a train in Russia and in the middle of nowhere, the train stopped. My family – the four of us – were in a cabin and I heard a loud knock at our door. It was pitch dark and I didn't know what was happening. At that time, the Russian mafia would stop trains because they knew people were travelling and they wanted to take everything from you – money, belongings, everything. In those days, Armenians would have gold teeth and the Russian mafia would open your mouth and pull your teeth out. And suddenly, they were at our cabin. I was on a bunk bed with my sister. Two men walked in and my dad stood up. They pointed a gun to his head saying in Russian, 'Give me everything you have.'

Luckily, because we were supposed to be going on holiday, we didn't take any valuables or jewellery with us because we would have been stopped and they would know we were trying to leave the country for good. So my dad said, 'We don't have anything.' And the guy didn't believe him, he kept pushing the gun to my dad's head. In our passports, there was a little error. Because they were stamped in a hurry, they were stamped incorrectly, and we knew that. When they checked our passports, if they had noticed, they could have deported us, but they didn't say anything. They just took our bags and when my dad emptied our four suitcases onto the floor, they saw we just had winter clothes. I was watching all of this. They didn't care about me and my sister. My mum was sitting there, stunned. When they realised we didn't have anything worth taking, they left. My dad actually had two gold teeth, but thankfully, they didn't look inside his mouth. I think they must have thought we were just poor and there was nothing to get from us. I had never seen my dad cry his entire life. He was 42 at the time we were in that train cabin – the age I am now – and he just sat down and started crying.

When we were living in Armenia, my dad became an alcoholic, but my mother always stood by him. They had both been through so much in their lives and my mum is such a strong woman – she never cried, not even on that train. As a child, I didn't really realise just what my parents must have gone through. It's only looking back now that I can see just how terrifying it all must have been for them.

When we finally arrived in Moscow after this fraught journey, we were passing a kiosk and my dad bought a Mars bar and Coca-Cola. He cut the bar into four slices and we all shared the bottle of Coke and chocolate. That was the first time in my life I tasted either of these iconic treats. I felt so trendy. Back in Armenia, only rich people would have those things. For us, that was a luxury. I remember eating that bar so slowly to savour it and make it last.

We continued on to a house that belonged to a friend of my aunt's. This was in January, three months after leaving Armenia. The house was very small and the four of us slept together on a mattress on the floor. I'd been to Moscow before but this was the first time I was scared for my life being there. We had no idea where we would end up next.

The next leg of the journey was by train to Cologne in Germany. It took two weeks. The train might stop to refuel before travelling another 48 hours straight, but we couldn't get off because of the type of tickets we had. We also weren't eating much because we couldn't afford food and had to ration our funds. In a 24-hour day, we'd have a small meal to share among the four of us. I was so skinny.

We arrived in Cologne and didn't know what to do next – how were we going to get to Denmark? We also didn't know anyone in Denmark, we were just heading there because of the visa we had. It was at this point that my dad said he would love to visit his brother before we continued on our journey. My uncle was living in Belgium and when we were in Armenia, he would send me these '80s tracksuits and I thought he must have been so successful – like, legit – but he was a refugee like us, waiting to get his papers.

As I was standing with my family in the train station wondering what to do next, luck entered my life again. A gentleman came over to my sister, thinking, *This poor child*, and gave her some money. It was enough to add to what we had to buy tickets to go to either Belgium or Denmark. It was fate – it was meant to be. We went to Belgium, where our new life was going to begin.

*****

Four months after leaving Armenia, we arrived at my uncle's home in Belgium. He had three kids of his own, and it was a small apartment. When we got there, my uncle said to us, 'You need to seek asylum.' We were going to be refugees.

The four of us went to the Petit Château – the famous 'Little Castle' in Brussels, which is a reception centre for political refugees. It was horrendous. There were mattresses on the floor and the first thing they did was grab us and put us on one of these mattresses while they decided our fate. Luckily, because we were a family who were together, not just individuals, the Salvation Army saw us and said, 'We'll help them.' In the Petit Château, there were loads of individuals, there were even cousins who were together, but they weren't taken in – the Salvation Army only took entire families.

We were sent to stay in a small room in the Salvation Army centre and I remember it was so clean and there was a double mattress on the floor for my parents and two single mattresses – one for me and another for my sister. And there on the table was a bottle of Diet Coke and some Jaffa Cakes wrapped in tin foil. After travelling for months, it felt to us like a palace.

There was an old television there so I grabbed the remote and started looking through the channels and on came *Baywatch*. That was the day I discovered Pamela Anderson. As a 13-year-old boy, I thought, *I am in love!* To this day, I am obsessed with her. We sat in complete silence watching *Baywatch*, not understanding a word of it, and a knock came at the door. A person came in with a box and put it on the table. My mum opened the box and inside was a razor. They said to her, 'You have to shave your kids' heads.' I don't know why it was only the kids and not adults, but she was told that every refugee who lived there had to shave their children's heads because of lice. It didn't matter that we didn't have lice, we had to just do what we were told. At the time, my mum spoke a little bit of English but couldn't speak French so communicating was really difficult for her, and my sister and I didn't understand anything that was being said. That night, Dad took out the razor and shaved our heads. I was mortified. I was bald and I hated it. I wore a cap for months.

That was the start of the whole procedure. We had to stay in our room. We weren't allowed to leave. Security had to be able to see you. If we went anywhere, we were afraid we'd be sent back to Armenia. I was young so I didn't understand why I couldn't go out to play. Men were allowed to go to the Petit Château and stand outside to find work for cash. The first day my dad went, he got work painting someone's house, and came home the following day with about €20 worth of Belgian francs. My mum and dad had to go to the government to explain why we were there, seeking asylum. They had to get their stories straight – if one piece of one person's story differed from the other's, you were out. They had to say they feared for their children's lives, that we were going to die if we stayed in Armenia. That's what they wanted to hear. We lived in that Salvation Army centre for four months, without ever seeing Brussels. And from there, they would decide where they would send us next because there were always more people coming in.

We were sent to Dinant, where there was a massive building that housed refugees from every country. I started going to school there and saw families come and go from that building – some were sent on a plane back to their home countries because they didn't get accepted. We lived there for three months and were the last refugees to stay in that building before it was demolished and replaced with apartments. We were then sent to live in a little apartment in Malmedy, which is near the German border of Belgium. I remember this lady, she was very energetic, who said to us in French, '*Vous devrez partir!* We have a house for you – you need to go.' We'd never heard of Malmedy. It was a very small village. And the irony of ironies was, here we were, a family of Armenians, and our new landlord was Turkish. (At the time, relations between Turkey and Armenia had long been problematic, especially after war broke out between Armenia and Azerbaijan.) When we met him, our new landlord said, 'You are Armenian?' Thankfully, he was the sweetest man. He and his family loved us, they cared for us, and they wanted to help us. It was a two-storey house and he lived there with his wife, son and daughter on the ground floor, while we lived in a small apartment upstairs.

We didn't know how long we'd be staying there but we didn't care – we just wanted to be safe. So that was our first real apartment in Belgium. And every week, my parents had to travel two hours each way by bus to Brussels to see the social worker. We just tried to build a life for ourselves while not knowing what was going to happen.

Back in Armenia, when she was younger, my mum was an opera singer for seven years. So she joined the Malmedy Cathedral choir and became the shining star. She quickly made friends. Everybody loved Maria. She was strong and opinionated and people started confiding in her. My dad, meanwhile, got a job in the Red Cross. He became well known in Malmedy because he helped everybody. Everybody knew Hakob – Hakob can fix this, Hakob can do that. My family became famous in Malmedy. We were the first-ever Armenian family there, so everyone got to know us. I started school but because I couldn't speak French, I was put in a class of seven people, who were all the naughty kids, because the school didn't know what else they could do with me. I remember in the class there was this mean girl, this bully, who looked like Brigitte Bardot – she was stunning. I couldn't afford to buy anything, so I was wearing clothes from the Red Cross that my dad would bring home. One day, she said, 'Oh, how disgusting – you're wearing my cousin's jacket that was donated. That's so tacky!' I went home and went crazy. I took my jacket and threw it on the floor. I was like, *I can't do this.*

The bullying only got worse. There were times I had glasses thrown at me. People spat at me. I had food thrown at me, like a dog. One time I was in a fast-food restaurant and someone threw a burger at me – like, you don't have any money, here, have some food. If I was in the cinema, the kids would see me, grab a popcorn container, fill it with popcorn from the floor and hand it to me, saying they'd bought it for me. The kids would say things they knew I wouldn't understand because I didn't fully know the language, so they could all laugh at me. I would never tell my mum – she'd already been through so much herself, I didn't want to worry or upset her. I'd just pretend I was fine. The person working in the school canteen would see me in the queue and wouldn't serve me, she'd help the person behind me instead. It wasn't always aggressive, obvious bullying – sometimes I was simply excluded. And I never fought back or said anything when it would happen. I was shy and embarrassed and afraid. I was terrified that if I were to react, I'd be deported back to Armenia. So I had to just take it, I couldn't do anything. I was just grateful to be somewhere safe with my family. There were nights when I'd be asleep in my bed and wake in a panic thinking I was back in Armenia. Eventually, I started making friends, and the people in the community were really nice to us, dropping by the house with food and wanting to help us in any way they could. The only thing was, at the end of the day, we were vulnerable. If the government didn't want us there anymore, there was nothing anyone could do to help us.

Then one day in 1995, when I was 15, I was spotted by a casting director from an agency in France who happened to be in Belgium. I always looked a bit androgynous, with a large nose and big ears: I looked a little weird. I was tall, skinny – completely different from Belgian boys with their blue eyes and small noses. I had been there a year by then, so I could speak a little bit of French. And he said, 'Are you a model?' And I told him no. He offered to bring me to Paris and said he'd give me a modelling scholarship.

I was so excited, I ran home to tell my mum. She was like, 'You're not going to Paris! You can't even leave the country!' Of course, I couldn't go anywhere because if I was stopped, I didn't have papers. So that idea went out the window, but that experience fuelled my desire to do something creative with my life.

My uncles were barbers back in Armenia, and I loved hair, so in September 1996, when I was 16, I decided to get into hairdressing and do an apprenticeship. We had moved to a new house that was bigger than the one owned by the Turkish landlord, and because we were in Belgium for nearly two years at this stage, my dad was allowed to work a certain amount of hours for earnings but he was very unhappy. If it weren't for us, I think he would have gone back to Armenia. He was a gentle soul – he never laid a hand on me – but he did have a strong presence that would sometimes make me feel timid around him.

One night that November, I awoke on the sofa – I don't know why I wasn't in my room – and my dad had just come home from work. He was in the kitchen eating dinner and he was talking to himself. I couldn't understand what he was saying. He was losing it. He went to bed that night and in the morning, my mum started screaming, saying, 'Oh my God, something's wrong.' I walked into the room and my dad's eyes were closed, but he was making this strange sound. We called an ambulance and went to the hospital. He'd had a brain haemorrhage and ended up in a coma for two and a half weeks. He was only alive because of the machines. There was a moment during that time in hospital when I was talking to my father and spotted what looked like a tear coming down his face. I thought he could hear me and was crying. That led the doctor to finally come in to see us. He could see we still had hope. He said, 'I know this is difficult ...' He explained that it wasn't a tear – it was just condensation as a result of the cold from the machines. The doctor went on, 'Listen, we did all the tests. If we switch this off, he's not alive. You need to make a decision.' That was the hardest thing my mum ever had to do – she had to give consent, she had to talk to my dad's brother to get his consent. Once they switched off the machines, he wasn't there anymore. My dad was gone. When that happened, something changed in me forever.

Because of the impact my dad had on the community, his funeral was the biggest Malmedy had ever seen. It was snowing and the queue was so long, it was as if a member of royalty had died. People walked in the snow from the house and the cathedral was packed. The locals said they had never seen anything like it in the village before.

We came home after the funeral and I was destroyed. I hated every single minute of it. I remember thinking, *what am I going to do?* My mum was distraught. We still didn't know if we could stay – we were still refugees, waiting. My dad's dream, all his life, was to see the Eiffel Tower, to go to Paris. He was 45 when he died and I just thought, *life is too short.* There are so many things I want to do. Before my father died, I was shy and afraid of everything. Now, I wasn't scared of anything … except not living the life I wanted to live.

Weeks later, we were clearing out Dad's wardrobe and Mum suddenly remembered something Dad told her just two days before he died. He'd cut a hole in the back of his wardrobe to hide his savings and wanted her to know in case anything ever happened. We took a look and there, in his secret hiding spot, we found a box filled with money. It was the equivalent of only a couple of hundred euro but he had worked hard to save that. Mum said, 'This money is no good to us. We're going to spend it. Life is too short.' I bought an electric razor so that I could shave my face and my sister bought a new dress: these were things we once thought we wouldn't ever have.

And then I said to my mum, 'I can't live here anymore.' She asked what I planned to do and I told her I was moving to Brussels. Because I was doing hairdressing, I was working in a salon four days a week while going to school, so I decided I'd go to school in Brussels, work in a salon, and find a place to live. I moved there on my own in February 1997. I was still just 16. I found a studio right in the city centre and got a job working in a hair salon.

After my father died, I made the decision that from then on, I would choose to do whatever I wanted – I had nothing to lose. I wanted my life to be incredible. It was very selfish – I left my mum and my sister behind. I should have been the man of the house, but I couldn't. If I had stayed there, I would have been depressed, and I don't think I would have survived in that house. And my mum knew – she saw it in my eyes. She said, 'Go! If you have to do this, go. I'll be there to support you.' Living in Brussels, I quickly landed on my feet. I was lucky – I was cute, I had thick, massive hair and I was full of energy. At the same time, I didn't really know what I was doing. I was still in my first year doing my apprenticeship so had to go back and forth as I had to finish my apprenticeship where I started. But I was determined – this was where my life would change. I took the train once a week to finish school and sometimes it was very hard because I couldn't afford the fares. My boss, who owned several salons, was very kind, though, and supported me.

Then one day in the salon I declared, 'I want to do celebrity hair.' My manager and colleagues just laughed. They were like, *yeah, right, of course you will.* So the next time I knew the boss was coming into the salon, I grabbed a mannequin and created this look that had everyone gobsmacked. Next thing, I was asked to assist with the hairdressing for the Eurovision qualifiers in Belgium, I was assisting stylists for catwalk shows, the Miss Belgium pageant and other events. All my life, people wouldn't take me seriously, but I was the new Arthur now. No one was going to stop me.

In May of 1997, six months after my dad died, we received a letter saying we had to leave Belgium. We were not accepted and would have to pack up and go. My mum's friend said to her, 'I know a man who lives two hours from here. He's single. You need to get married. You need help.' My mum was like, 'I can't do that. I don't know this man.' So her friend advised her to meet him and just start dating.

My mum was two years older than my dad and was around 30 when my parents got married – my dad was actually married before and I have a half-sister who lives in LA, but his first wife left because she had a difficult relationship with my grandmother. When she met Paul in the summer of 1997, my mum was about 49. Paul Caro was from Sprimont in Belgium. His wife had passed away the same month and year as my dad and he didn't have any children. He was such a nice man. He was a retired teacher in his mid-fifties, petite and skinny, and my mum was so powerful next to him. The two of them met and started dating, had a real connection, and a couple of months later, Paul said, 'You are an incredible woman. You are not going anywhere. Marry me.' It was his idea – she never asked him for help. I think he just wanted her companionship and knew about our situation. They married before I turned 18, so I got a Belgian passport straight away and we were all able to stay in Belgium. My mum had to wait two years for her passport but she didn't care – she did that for us. She said to my sister and me, 'If it weren't for you two, I would have gone back to Armenia by now.' Paul was wonderful – before they married, he used to drive two hours to Malmedy to visit my mother. After they got married, they travelled across Europe together and really enjoyed life. Then, just two years after they married, Paul had a haemorrhage, became paralysed and was in a wheelchair for the rest of his life. My mother looked after Paul for the next 13 years. To her, that man saved our lives and she was going to care for him until the day he died. He passed away in 2011. Paul was so good to my mother, my sister and me. If I struggled to pay my rent in Brussels, he would help me out. He was so kind and generous and treated me like one of his own. I will never forget everything he did for us.

*****

I finished hairdressing training when I was 19. This was the start of a new chapter in my life, where dancing would play a central role. I started going to nightclubs. I wasn't interested in alcohol or drugs – I just wanted to dance and have fun.

One night, in December 1999, I was dancing with my hairdressing friends in a nightclub in Antwerp called Café d'Anvers. A woman came up to me and asked, 'Are you a dancer?' When I said no, she said, 'Come with me.' I didn't know what was happening. At this point in time, I didn't know I was gay. I thought she was hitting on me, and she was pretty, so I followed her and suddenly I realised, this is where the dancers who worked in the club go, why are we here? She led me up the stairs and opened this door and it was like something out of a movie, like a mirage. I was blown away – boom! I couldn't believe my eyes. There before me were all the dancers, stretching, applying make-up; there were feathers and costumes. She turned to me and said, 'One of our dancers couldn't make it tonight, he's been delayed, and I need a boy to fill the spot. You're the only one I saw out there who can move. Dance on a platform, and your friends can have free drinks all night.' I was like, *Hell yeah!* In those days, go-go dancing in nightclubs was huge. You could make so much money just dancing on a platform in the corner of the club. I didn't know these dancers got paid so well when I said yes – I was just so happy to dance, and knowing my friends were looked after was a bonus. She gave me these massive white wings to wear and a pair of the teeniest, tiniest shorts. She said, 'Go out on that platform and just do whatever you want.' My knees were shaking. I stepped onto the platform and the music and lights signalled the moment when the dancers would change. There I was, topless with these huge wings, with around a hundred people staring at me. I saw my friends looking up at me with an expression on their faces like, what are you *doing* up there? And I just thought, *what's the worst that can happen?* I just started dancing. I was living my best life.

When I finished, early in the morning, the woman handed me the equivalent of about €100. I asked, 'Why are you giving me money?' She's like, 'You were working – people get paid to work.' I thought I was just doing this for free, for fun! I said to her, 'Next week, same time?' She replied, 'Are you a dancer?' I said, 'I could be!' She stared at me from head to toe, toe to head and said, 'Okay, I'll call you next week.' I don't remember her name, and never saw that woman ever again but she looked like Pamela Anderson. The following week, I got a call from a man named Cliff. He explained that the woman gave him my number and asked if I was free the following Saturday night. I told him I'd be there. The next week, I walked into this other club in Antwerp. Again, at this point in my life, I didn't know I was gay. I had no experience of the LGBTQ+ community. I looked around and only saw men in the club. I asked, 'When are all the people coming, where are all the girls?' It was the first time I'd ever been inside a gay club. It was a very famous club called Red & Blue. The guy looked at me and said, 'Are you kidding? This is a gay bar.' I was like, 'What do you mean?' My heart started pounding. I was thinking, *I'm dead. I'm Armenian ... my family, what would they say?* At this point in time, being gay was still illegal in Armenia – it was decriminalised later, in 2003 – and to this day, it's still not generally accepted there by society. I prayed there was no one in that club who might recognise me. I'd be in so much trouble if anyone found out.

Once again, I was given this skimpy outfit to wear and I was dancing with a shower raining down on me in front of a roomful of gay men. All eyes were on me and I was loving it. I was the new kid on the block. That's when everything started for me. I told my mum I was now dancing in nightclubs. And everyone said to me, 'That's not real dancing.' But I proved everybody wrong. I was booked to dance in one of the biggest nightclubs in Europe – Zillion in Antwerp – in front of six thousand people. I felt like the king of the world and I was game for anything. And the money I was making – I never thought I could actually earn that much. Whether this lasted one minute or one million minutes, I was in it for the ride.

I no longer wanted to work in the salon because I'd be dancing all night. My boss agreed to keep me on for catwalk and TV work. He wouldn't do that for anyone else.

*****

In Armenia, you're brought up to believe you'd get married young and have kids. I didn't even know that it was possible for two men to be together, so it never occurred to me that I was gay. Then I found myself dancing in a gay club, seeing men together and I was beginning to understand it. I started taking a dance class when I was 20 and there was a guy there who was five years older than me. We started hanging out. I didn't exactly fancy him – I wasn't really paying attention, and I was dating a girl, a ballerina. After a couple of months, I randomly said to him, 'Let me cut your hair.' We went for a drink first and he was flirting with me without me realising it. He came back to my studio and I was cutting his hair. He was topless and suddenly I felt myself blushing and out of the blue, I said to him, 'Can I kiss you?' I will never forget that feeling. He said yes and I kissed him and I immediately thought, *no, this is disgusting.* It went against everything I was brought up to believe. He told me not to worry, it's okay. And I just said, 'I'm sorry, it's just I've never done this before.' And he said, 'But you're gay.' And I said, 'What do you mean? I don't know what you're talking about. I have a girlfriend.' He said, 'Listen, I know you're in denial, but trust me.' Shortly afterwards, I broke up with my girlfriend. She was so upset but I knew it was the right thing to do. I started dating that guy and three months later, my friends found out, but I told them all I was bisexual.

I suppose deep down I was always gay but just didn't know or understand it and once I accepted that, I wasn't going to hide it – I had to be myself. So I knew I had to tell my mum and my sister. I didn't care what anyone else thought. By the time I felt ready to tell my mum, my aunt Anya – Mum's sister – was dying of cancer. I went to the hospital to say goodbye and was sitting beside my aunt's bed. I couldn't comprehend what was happening, I just wanted it out, so I said to my mum, 'There's something I need to tell you. I'm with a guy.' Her eyes filled with tears and she was livid and confused. She was losing her sister and I was coming out to her all at once. She said in a low voice, 'We'll talk about this later. This is not right. That's not you. Who told you you were like that?' I got up to walk out of the room and as I was leaving, I heard my aunt say to my mum, 'Don't worry about me – go save your son.' Even on her deathbed, my aunt thought it was more important for my mother to rescue me than be by her sister's side – that my being gay must be a sign I was having some sort of episode and needed help, that I needed saving from this path I was on. My aunt died and the following day, my mum came to see me to talk things over. She begged me to leave my boyfriend, worried what people would think, and I refused. I felt good being with him, I felt comfortable. It was the first and last time I was ever harsh with my mother. I said, 'You don't know what you're talking about. I'm staying with him.' She was so hurt and we didn't speak for a year. That was the hardest time. We were so close and suddenly we weren't in contact. I tried to reach out to my sister, but she was 18 and couldn't understand what was going on. She kept saying, 'How are people going to react? What are they going to say about us?' They were particularly worried about what my uncle in Belgium would think.

Then in June 2001, my boyfriend organised a party for my 21st birthday and my mum turned up. She ran up to me crying and said she didn't care that I was gay, she just asked me not to tell the rest of our family. I said I'd play the game and pretended to be straight to all of my Armenian relatives to make her happy and, little by little, my mother grew not only to accept me but to better understand who I was. We've been the best of friends ever since.

Later that summer, I broke up with that boyfriend and, armed with my new passport, I left Belgium to see what else – and who else – was out in the world waiting for me to discover.

3

BRIAN:

London

n 1998, I made the move to Bishop's Stortford near Stansted Airport to work as an air steward with Ryanair. I was ready for adventure and to discover who I was without the eyes of everyone in Rathangan watching.

Before I left, Mum gave me everything that was in her bank account. It was £300. She said, 'That's all I can give you, it's all we have until next week.' I didn't understand what she meant. I was 20, I was moving away and I was leaving behind my six sisters, who were all living at home, with my mother having to figure out how she was going to stretch the budget another week. When I think about that now, I'm amazed at the sacrifices my parents made for me.

Living in Stansted, I read *Time Out* magazine, looking through the section featuring gay bars and clubs, and I'd go out and explore them on my own. I'd see guys kissing each other and wonder, is this me? I remember my first kiss with a guy in a nightclub. I was like, *Alright, this feels okay.* Then he turned to another guy next to him and said, 'Oh yeah, this is my boyfriend.' And that sense of shame came rushing back. I left the club thinking, *I'm a whore. I've kissed this guy and he has a boyfriend. What have I done?*

Then I found myself a tribe. We were a group of six – three guys and three girls – and we'd take the train from Stansted Airport to Liverpool Street station with a naggin of vodka in the bag and cans of Red Bull (I had by now discovered I actually liked the taste of alcohol, so long as it came mixed up in a delicious package). We'd then hop on the Tube and hit the clubs and stay out until four o'clock in the morning before clubbing our money together – ten quid each – to get a taxi home. I'd queue outside London's iconic G-A-Y nightclub to see S Club 7, B*Witched or Westlife – all these people I would end up meeting or working with years later – the Vengaboys, Kylie Minogue … I'd go up to the doorman and blag my way in, saying something like, 'Karen Miller from Calvin Klein put us on the guest list … Yeah, we're definitely on there.' And they'd let us in!

I thought my life couldn't get any better. My friends and I were all the same age; some were straight, some were bisexual, some were gay. We were all so accepting of each other and would head out together to gay bars, straight bars, drag shows, and even holidays. I suppose we were kind of naive to the world. We were all living away from home for the very first time, trying new things and having fun.

I was able to freely explore my sexuality while living in the UK, to be two very different people: gay Brian, who'd go out, be curious, have one-night stands with no judgement from anyone; and then I'd go home to Ireland and back to being Brian who was in the closet. I wouldn't say I was straight, but I wasn't being open or talking about myself. And I was never asked, not by my parents or my sisters. When I was home, which was pretty often, I wouldn't be as sassy or shining as brightly as I would be when I was out with my friends in London. I would rein it in. In London, I could explore Soho and the gay scene and not feel guilt or worry. There was no shame. I was surrounded by people who didn't judge me or anyone else.

Back then, the type of men I found attractive were usually slightly older than me, with money or good jobs. That probably stemmed from the fact that I grew up with little money. I'd get compliments from men – I was young, had a great personality, an Irish accent and greenish-blue eyes, so it was easy to get free drinks on a night out.

When I met my first serious boyfriend, Keith, I fell really hard. He was eight years older than me, an investment banker from Edinburgh, privately educated and so different from me. We were together when I got an application form for *Big Brother* and he didn't want me to apply – he said it was degrading for anyone to be seen on television brushing their teeth or taking a shower. Despite our feelings for one another, we were so incompatible – we came from two very different worlds, so we broke up. I was hurt by it as it felt like love at the time, but we just didn't work. I watched some of the first season of *Big Brother* with Nick Bateman and Anna Nolan, thinking, *Anna's Irish, she's gay, she was a nun, wow!* I got an application form for the second season, but hesitated to fill it in. Then Keith messaged me on Valentine's Day 2001 saying, 'No roses for you this year.' That fuelled a fire in me. Raging, I filled in the form and sent it off. Keith and I ended up getting back together just before I went on the show. I wanted something safe to return to when I came out of the house. We kept our relationship super-quiet. That was my decision – somehow I knew, even at the age of 22, that I wanted to keep that private, and we got away with that, too. No one knew I had a boyfriend.

Before I went into the *Big Brother* house, my sister Michelle told me she thought I needed to come out to my parents. I think she always knew I was gay, even though I never told her outright – we were just so close. It's funny, you don't think anyone knows. I was too afraid to tell my parents myself so I asked Michelle if she would do it for me. When I asked her later how our parents took the news, she said they were a bit surprised but didn't really ask questions. The next day, I rang Mum and she said to me, 'Are you trying to be fashionable?' And I said, 'Mum, if I was trying to be fashionable, I would just buy a really nice jumper.' And that was it. Two days later, I entered the *Big Brother* house.

On the cover of one of the tabloids was a picture of me that someone had sold to the publication. It was taken at a Halloween party, and the photo was of me with four other guys dressed as the Spice Girls. I was Posh Spice. The whole cover of that tabloid was of me with the headline: 'Queer we go again' because Anna Nolan was in the first season. That really hurt my mum and she took to the bed for two days. I had catapulted my parents into a situation where we had photographers and reporters outside their gate, but their loyalty, love and support never faltered. There was a pub in Rathangan that screened the first show and I was completely nude in the shower, bum hanging out. Back then, my parents didn't have cable television, so when the nominations would air live, someone would ring my mum and tell her I wasn't up for eviction, and she could relax.

When I finally came out of the house as the winner on 27 July 2001, I immediately went to hug my mum and that was the first time she embraced me as my authentic self, as her openly gay son. That moment was so priceless, I'd forgotten about the £70,000 prize. I didn't even realise there were fireworks going off to my left and right.

That was such a long walk. I remember meeting Davina McCall halfway and she rubbed my face and said to me, 'It's all for you. This is all for you.' And I just kept saying, 'Where is my mum?' I remember hugging Mum and asking her about my sister Tracey, who was 17 and 8 months pregnant at the time with my niece Chloe. Then I was whisked away to do the interview with Davina. When I look back at that interview now, I was just stunned. I turned 23 in the house. I could not believe everything around me. These people were chanting my name. I could see my family – Aoife was nine at the time and Tara was six and they ran towards me and security jumped in and tried to stop them. And I went, 'No, they're my sisters. What are you doing?' Then I was dragged away into a room to see a psychologist and do a debrief and I didn't see my family again for another two weeks.

I was being celebrated for being the winner of *Big Brother*, which made my coming out a pretty positive experience. I always joked with Mum, 'Even if you disagreed with me being gay or had any issues, what could you say? I won the show!' Everyone's coming-out story is so individual to them. I have such respect for kids who are 12, 13, 14 … in school being authentic and out and proud. It's so brave and we need to celebrate that more.

*****

There was, however, another very dark side to all of that. I had the same mobile phone from when I was working in Ryanair when I was out of the *Big Brother* house and back in the real world. Loads of people had that number and when I went to listen to my messages, the amount of death and rape threats and abuse waiting for me was crippling: 'You're a disgusting faggot,' 'We're going to rape you and give you AIDS,' 'We'll find you – we know you're in London.' There were so many messages of hate from men practically spitting through the phone and being so aggressive, threatening my life and saying what they were planning to do to me. I couldn't understand it and never told anyone because I was so embarrassed. I wondered, *is this my fault or is this normal?* I'd never experienced anything like that before. It was very shocking and I couldn't wait to change my number. I signed with an agent, got a phone in someone else's name and had security for a few weeks. I didn't want anyone to have my new number. The abuse was just dreadful and so scary. I felt so violated.

I moved in with Keith, not because we wanted to live together, but we were kind of forced into it because I knew I had to be in London for work. Then, all I had in London was Keith. My friends were all back in Stansted. My family was in Ireland. I was only 23 years old and it was all so chaotic. I thought because I'd won the show, people would only be saying nice things about me, but that wasn't always the case. When I'd go to gay bars after winning *Big Brother*, there were other gay men there who hated me and would push me or throw drinks in my face because I was projecting a stereotype that wasn't accurate – not all gay men are effeminate or like Destiny's Child. I used to love wearing crop tops, but I was just being myself. Looking back, I probably didn't help the situation by being arrogant or rude at times, but while in some ways that was the happiest time for me, there were really horrible moments of feeling traumatised by everything mentally, being so young, having no one close to me in London, and just on this hamster wheel.

To others, it probably looked like I was comfortable. I'd become quite good at faking it over the years. We all pretend that everything is okay, don't we? It's funny what fame does; others don't see you as a regular person. The thing about being famous is, you don't really change as a person – it's the people around you in different situations who do. I remember thinking none of it was real, and it could all be taken away at any point. I didn't know if my 15 minutes of fame would be a week, two weeks, a year or more. I had planned to go back to Ryanair at the start of September. It was only when I got a deal with a production company that wanted to make a documentary that I changed that plan. I never went back to working in an airline, but even a month after the show, I thought I'd be going back to my normal job, doing normal things. Fame at that level, it's very odd. My experience all came down to being on telly for nine weeks, living in a bubble, and suddenly my life had changed and I'd won more money than I thought I'd ever be able to save up in my entire life. Before all of this, my account was always overdrawn.

After *Big Brother*, things were so intense. I was dragged absolutely everywhere. The club I used to blag my way into, G-A-Y, wanted to do a welcome home party for me.

I thought, *this is the club I used to queue outside of in the rain and lie to get into*. I had to go on stage, and the crowd was packed in. I had security and couldn't mix with people because they said it'd be dangerous, so I sat by myself with two security guards, drinking a Bacardi Breezer through a straw. I remember thinking, I don't want this. I want to be dancing to S Club 7.

I'd be going into these places through the kitchens, people were giving false names. There were photographers running around and chasing us in cars. It all seemed so silly to me because I didn't see the big deal. I realised later, what these photographers wanted was to get me with my boyfriend because there were rumblings that I had someone. I don't think anyone really gets used to fame, not at that level. Quickly enough, though, I copped on to the fact that this was what I had to do to earn money, that my currency was my body and my personality.

That said, I've always had an issue with being touched or people invading my personal space. I think it goes back to that teacher in primary school who slapped me across the face in front of a roomful of peers. It's always made me hugely uncomfortable.

When I was an air steward, I had my ass slapped and pinched, and my crotch grabbed numerous times a week by predominantly straight men on stag weekends who'd see me, an air steward, and assume I'd love it. I remember one passenger tried to handcuff me to one of the doors down the back of the aircraft – this was pre-9/11, so people were able to bring all sorts of things on board then. I had to physically fight him off and shout for help.

In my private life and relationships, I've been with men who didn't like the word no. And it's only when I look back now that I think, why didn't I have the confidence to remove myself from those situations? Or simply say, 'No, I'm uncomfortable.' I'm naturally flirty and chatty, and the first time I experienced something like that was at an after-party – I went to the bathroom and hadn't locked the door and a guy followed me in, locked the door behind him and started touching and kissing me. I was like, 'What are you doing?' And he said, 'Come on, we were chatting and you were giving me the eye.' And for a split second, I thought, *did I? Maybe I did?* Then something inside me suddenly went, 'Get out. Get away from me.' That was when I decided I needed to stand up for myself more. Those feelings of people putting their hands on you never leave you. And I've always felt the work that I do – being in the public eye and accessible – you'd make public appearances at clubs and for want of a better word, you are a piece of meat, you're being paid to go in there, and you are grabbed and pulled. I had to learn to create more boundaries.

*****

Looking back over those years, I can say now that the inappropriateness I had to deal with, the lines people crossed on jobs, stuff that was said to me and things I experienced were not okay. But back then, I presumed it was normal and just something I had to go along with.

I began co-hosting *SMTV Live* with Tess Daly in 2002. It was the biggest kids' TV show in the UK, it aired every Saturday and here I was, an openly gay man, as their new anchor. At 23, I didn't understand what that meant. I remember someone saying to me, 'People know you're gay, they've just never seen you being gay.' I thought, *what does that mean?* What that meant was, I couldn't go on a red carpet with a guy. I had to go with Tess or a friend. I couldn't be seen in photographs looking romantic with a man. But I could be on *SMTV Live* playing a camp character or alluding to my gayness in a sketch in a way that would go over the children's heads. And now I wonder why I, and the people I worked with, allowed that. I remember on more than one occasion during a studio rehearsal, a straight man would approach me, put his hand over my face, maybe holding a tissue but sometimes with his bare hand, and aggressively rub my lips shouting, 'Stop wearing lipstick.' And I'd go, 'I'm not – my lips are just this colour.' He presumed because I was gay and my lips were bright red, I must be wearing make-up. I had heterosexual men picking out my wardrobe with a stylist because my clothes couldn't look gay. They couldn't reflect anything of me, and I thought this was normal. I didn't realise that it was wrong.

Back then, there was no social media, so I had to actively get out and be on every red carpet there was going. I'd go to openings and premieres. You had to be in magazines every single week. Working on *SMTV Live* involved a rehearsal on Thursday and Friday and you'd do the show on Saturday, but every day, you'd be doing something to promote the show. And the hustle – push, push, push. I was quite thin then, with dark circles under my eyes. I was anaemic, too. I also used to go on sunbeds a lot so I'd always have a tan. I remember being told by production people to go to the gym. Hearing all of that did lead me to have issues with my body. Looking at other gay men, and what they looked like – the boy bands and heart throbs who'd appear on the show each week, they'd all have six packs and I'd be wondering why I didn't look like that. I just never had that kind of body, and that used to really upset me. So I wouldn't eat.

*****

In May of that year, Keith moved to Australia, so we broke up, and I was living on my own in his house in Clapham. I went to visit him that November, which brought final closure to our relationship, so when I got back to London, I knew we were truly done. We always pre-recorded the *SMTV Live* episode that aired after Christmas the week before and we taped the show on a Friday morning, so that night, I went to The Shadow Lounge with my best friend Simon Jones, who works in PR – he was my first publicist – his brother Spencer, and Spencer's girlfriend at the time. We were dancing, and I looked over and saw this gorgeous guy. He was wearing a green T-shirt that had the word 'army' on it. I turned to Simon and said, 'Oh my God.' Simon encouraged me to go up to him so I walked over and said hello. The music was loud but he just shrugged and said, 'No English.' I walked back to my friends and said, 'He can't speak English.' Simon was like, 'So? It's one night, what do you care?' And I was like, 'You're totally right.' I went back over and we started chatting. He told me his name was Arthur and I told him I worked in PR – a little fib to avoid him clocking who I was – and he said he was a dancer. I said, 'Yeah, of course you're a dancer. Half the guys in this club are dancers.' I was drinking Smirnoff Ice and was going through my hot phase then – my hair was short, I was skinny and I had a tan. But I couldn't get over how attractive Arthur was. I was mesmerised. He oozed sexiness – I knew he was better looking than me and way more confident.

We went back to my place and snogged and I remember him saying to me, 'You need to slow down with the kissing.'

I think he actually thought I was a dreadful kisser. From the beginning, I felt there was something to Arthur that was very different from other guys I'd been with, and I knew I wanted to see him again. We exchanged numbers and over the coming days, we texted each other.

A week or so later, I was in the studio, walking beside Tess Daly, and suddenly I spotted the guy from the night-club sitting at a table in the canteen. I was like, *what is he doing here?* It turned out, he was dancing on *CD:UK* with Zoe Birkett, who'd been on *Pop Idol*. Tess and I had such a great relationship, so I wanted her opinion. I was like a 16-year-old schoolgirl. She was like, 'Oh, honey, he is hot!' Of course, Arthur didn't know who I really was so I later had to explain why I was in that studio, that I was a TV presenter and was on a reality show before that. Arthur never watched *Big Brother* and it was reassuring for me that when I met him, he thought I was attractive. It felt so nice to meet someone who was genuinely interested in me.

We started dating, and I remember wanting to wait a while before getting too intimate and not rush things because I just knew there was something different about him. With Arthur, I wanted to make things special.

Then on Valentine's Day 2003, less than two months after we'd met, we were in my apartment and Arthur told me he was falling in love with me. I told him to get out. I said, 'What are you on about? No, I'm sorry.' I wasn't in that place yet and I was thrown. My friend who was there with me that night got up and said to me, 'Are you mad? He's just told you he's falling in love with you. This is everything. He's fantastic. What's wrong with you?' It was raining and I followed Arthur out onto the street and I couldn't find him. I started to cry, and thought to myself, *what has you so messed up that you have a guy you're clearly attracted to telling you he loves you and you go and break his heart?* All that stuff I'd been listening to about not being allowed to have a boyfriend – I think that was what had me so scared. I'd be out with Arthur on dates and men would come up and ask if I had a boyfriend and I'd say no. It was dreadful. I humiliated Arthur. I called him a few days later and eventually he agreed to take me back but while we both felt strongly for one another, those obstacles still kept getting in the way of our relationship.

At that time, Davina McCall was hosting a dating show called *Streetmate*, where you'd go out on the street and look for someone to date. Myself and Emma Bunton were doing it for Children in Need. *SMTV Live* didn't want me shooting that show – it would look like I was cruising the streets for gay men. In reality, it was nothing like that. *Streetmate* was so lovely, and I was doing it with Baby Spice for a good cause. I did the show and Arthur and I were still dating at that time. When the show aired, *Heat* magazine ran a cover story of me pictured with the person I went on the date with, who happened to be a model, and it appeared as though this was the new man in my life. Arthur was never a jealous person, but I know he would have been hurt by that, not because, there was anything actually going on but because, once again, he was pushed to the side like he didn't exist. I remember *SMTV Live* weren't happy with that magazine cover either. I kind of understood their concern, but at the same time, I didn't.

In 2004, I bought my first apartment on Abbeville Road in Clapham. It was so lovely. I loved my postcode – SW4. I was so proud and those walls saw so many memories made over the next 14 years. I was very fortunate to have so much success at such a young age, but equally it came with a lot of drama along the way. Meanwhile, in those first few years we were together, Arthur and I would break up and get back together several times. He'd move into that Clapham apartment and then pretty soon, he'd be moving out again. Every time I'd be on the cusp of feeling like I was ready to move on, he'd re-enter my life and we'd be back together. During all those break-ups, if I'd see Arthur with another guy, I'd move my way in and suggest we meet up and the guy would likely feel a little threatened, but I didn't care.

Then in 2006, Arthur was like, 'This is toxic. This just doesn't work.' He said he deserved better and walked out the door. After he left, I looked out the window onto Abbeville Road, watching him walk away, and I collapsed to the ground. I knew immediately I had just made one of the biggest mistakes of my life. Pride can be a horrible thing. I wanted to say, 'Don't go! I love you, please don't leave me.' But my pride wouldn't let me. I couldn't let him know I needed him. I don't know what it was, maybe it was my fight or flight response, but Arthur was gone from my life and I didn't know what I was going to do without him. What followed was five years of me trying to get over him … and almost getting there.

I went out one day and bought a Gucci ring for Arthur and gave it to him. In return, he gave me a two-page letter explaining why we wouldn't be getting back together. I still had high hopes that we'd be together eventually, though, and over the next five years we'd hang out, but would lie to our friends about it because they were sick of our dramas and didn't want to see us hurt each other anymore. But I liked that I still had that pull with Arthur, that something kept bringing him back to me, that he might still be interested.

My friends would say to me, 'Brian, you have to get over him.' I was absolutely broken. It was almost like a death. I grieved Arthur hard for maybe two years. And every time I'd see him out with a boyfriend, a part of me would die. I'd lose my breath and would need to take a minute to regroup. I always thought of Arthur as the one that got away. I felt he'd never really seen me at my full potential – he never got me at my best. He'd seen the arrogant version of me. At that time, everything I was doing was about work and it bled into my relationship: I didn't have the maturity or confidence to handle all of that. Arthur was everything I wanted – I just couldn't show him then.

I wasn't ready. There was so much I needed to do myself. I had to grow up. I had to lose him to know what I really wanted.

Then in July 2011, we met up for dinner and Arthur said I looked really good. He must have seen a growth in me. At that point, I thought I had moved past it, but he suggested we go out on a date. And when we kissed, it felt very new. We didn't tell anyone we were going out until October. It was nice to be secretly dating while we got to know each other again in private. Once we made it official, though, Simon and all my friends were quite worried. They'd be like, 'Where is this going?' because our big break-up was so sad the first time and they didn't want to see us go down that road again. But I said to Arthur from day one, 'If we're in this, we're in this.' This time, it was real and we were both determined to make it last.

*****

But while my relationship was finally back on track, my career was once again becoming a source of emotional stress. When I won *Ultimate Big Brother* in September

2010, and *Big Brother* was finishing on Channel 4, Davina McCall passed me her microphone. And just like when she rubbed my face in 2001, saying, 'It's all for you', I gestured to the audience and said to her, 'That's all for you.' She was the queen of *Big Brother*. I would never have thought a year later I'd be saying, 'Big Brother house, this is Brian. You're live on Channel 5.' I tested for that show alongside Emma Willis, but I didn't want the main show – I wanted the spin-off show because I knew I could cut my teeth there. I knew I could be myself. I could have more fun. I got offered the main show and straight away, it was almost as if the things I excelled at were the things I couldn't be doing anymore. If I wanted to turn left, I was told to turn right. Once again, there were inappropriate things said to me – I was told my accent was too Irish, I was too camp. Someone was brought in to show me how to walk more like a man. It was so degrading. When the show was announced, we did a promo, and I remember getting a message saying, 'You are so effeminate, no one's ever going to take you seriously. This is not how a primetime TV host operates.' I'd spoken to people about it and was told to shut up, that this was the greatest job and financially rewarding, that I should suck it up. I was tanning two or three times a week to stay bronzed, and I was overeating because I was so uncomfortable and unhappy. When I started hosting that show in 2011, I was really thin from working out excessively; by the start of 2013, I'd gained so much weight from binge eating – my coping mechanism to mask my emotions.

And then I was fired in 2013. That was the lowest I'd ever felt in my career. People get fired, it happens, but this was such a public shaming, and I felt so betrayed by everyone. It was humiliating. There was no duty of care. No one contacted me from Channel 5. Thank goodness I had Arthur – we'd just moved in together that year, and that was a great distraction – he was so supportive. But that was the darkest I'd felt in my life. There was so much written about me, rejoicing in my demise. Even when I was on the show, people would write things about me. Boyd Hilton was a TV critic for *Heat* magazine, and pictured beside his words was a cut-out of my head in a bin. My mum saw that and was horrified. Others would write or say things like, 'He shouldn't be the host.' I remember reading all of that, feeling awful, and Simon suggested the two of us go away to Mykonos. Then people saw me leaving the country and it was almost a joke – 'he's flying away from it all,' they said. It was just a horrible time. Even as I'm writing these words, I feel guilty for the people that did this to me. I feel sorry for them. I don't know why that is. Is it just the way I've been programmed? Like I feel bad for that person. Why am I blaming them? Maybe they were right. Maybe if I didn't have such an Irish accent, maybe if I wasn't so camp, maybe if I walked in a more masculine way …

No one cared what happened to me. I never received flowers or champagne. I never received anything from anyone – from the production, from the channel … Just two crew members from the show contacted me. The whole experience nearly broke me. I couldn't really work after that for a while. I'd be offered jobs and I wouldn't take them. I had no confidence, I lost my mojo. I was completely beaten down. It took a while to bounce back from that. I don't think that insecurity and vulnerability ever leave you. What I realised was, no one cares: I can be replaced. Anyone can be replaced. That was a valuable lesson to learn, and I think my whole work ethic changed from that.

*****

Right between getting the *Big Brother* job and losing it, I found myself in another dark and scary situation. It was February 2012 and Arthur was away working so I went down to Blockbuster Video to pick up a DVD, prepared for a quiet night in on my own. I stopped off at a cash point and took out £200 then walked back up Clapham High Street and down Cavendish Road. There's a gorgeous church there that you could see from my roof terrace. I was literally 20 seconds from my home when two guys approached me and one of them suddenly held a knife to my throat. The other one said, 'Don't move, don't say anything.' My immediate thought was that I was being kidnapped. I was wearing tracksuit bottoms and I could feel them both grabbing my crotch and bum because they were searching my pockets. Once again I was being touched in a way that made me feel excruciatingly uneasy. I had my phone, wallet, cash and house keys. I worried they were planning on dragging me towards my apartment or back to the cash machine – I could handle losing more cash, but what I really dreaded was them coming into my home. Did they recognise me and know who I was?

I remember so vividly the feeling of the knife to my throat. The man was holding my arms back and I could see people walking on the opposite side of the road but I couldn't scream for help. I was numb. Then they told me to stay still on the pavement until they were well out of sight. I did as they asked because I was afraid for my life. When they were gone, I ran up to the apartment. I was hysterical. I rang Arthur from the landline (as they'd taken my phone), then rang 999. The police came and asked if I thought it was a personal attack and I said no because they hadn't mentioned my name. The police suspected these men probably followed me after seeing me get cash on my own. They put me in the back of their car and we drove around the area looking for the two men. They asked me to describe them, but it was dark and truthfully, I didn't look at them – I was too afraid to make eye contact.

Then Simon rang me saying he got a call from someone, a reporter, who told him I'd been arrested because they saw me getting into a police car. I told him I was actually mugged, but I couldn't believe how quickly word got back to my PR. Then there were photographers outside my door the next day, and I realised then that people like me, who are in the public eye, are just a source of news, and living in London, you never really know if someone is watching you while you're going about your day-to-day life. You expect to have your picture taken when you're out at a club or on the red carpet, but it never occurred to me before that someone would be standing outside my apartment ready to catch me in the back of a police car. I was surprised people cared, if I'm honest.

*****

From the time Arthur and I got back together, I dropped so many hints about wanting to get married. There was a lot of pressure on him. In July 2014, we went to the Dominican Republic for a holiday. Arthur kept trying to suggest we do all this weird stuff like take a helicopter ride and I kept shooting down all these ideas, saying they were a waste of money or too dangerous. One of these sugges-tions was that we should hire a boat and I reminded him that I couldn't swim. Like, that is not happening. By the end of the trip, I was covered in mosquito bites. I had lumps on my neck and arms. I looked like Quasimodo. It was two days before we were due to go home and we returned to our room from the beach and when I opened the door, I saw there was a swan and loads of rose petals all over the bed, and I said, 'Oh my God, what's wrong with the staff at this hotel? Do they think we're on our honeymoon?' And then I spotted a drumstick on the bed with a ring on it next to a card (Arthur really loves the drums). I turned the card over and it said, 'Marry me'. I turned around and Arthur was on his knee. I was like, 'Are you actually serious?' I started to cry, and he just said, 'Will you marry me?'

We kissed and when I hugged him, I could see myself in the bathroom mirror and this is going to sound so silly, but I gave myself a thumbs-up. I couldn't help it. I was just so delighted. I thought to myself, you've actually done it – you've got the man you've always wanted. He was my Plan A+, my dream. I fought tooth and nail over the years, beating off competition from guys who were younger and who I believed were better looking than me. But at the end of the day, they weren't me. Arthur always loved me. He'd always say I was the only one who could make him laugh.

And I got the guy I never had to second guess myself with, the one I felt most comfortable with, who listened to me and loved my opinions, who wanted the best for me. I got the man who could see so much in me when I couldn't see it for myself. So while I'm a little mortified to admit to the thumbs-up at my reflection, which Arthur won't know about until he's read this book, that will tell you just how proud and exhilarated I felt at that moment. The ring, he explained, was his father's wedding band, and it was only temporary to use in that moment and we'd go out and choose our rings together. And I couldn't wait to start the next phase of our lives together.

4

ARTHUR:

From Europe to the UK

The next year was a whirlwind for me – I never stayed in one place for long. When I left Belgium in 2001, I went to Paris first for a couple of months. I had to see the Eiffel Tower for my dad. Then I went to the coast of Spain for another two months because I was on tour. Once again, I was living in a place where I didn't understand the language, and there wasn't much for me to do there. I got a call to audition back in Paris for the musical *Notre-Dame de Paris*. They were casting dancers. I didn't get it, but the choreographer said to me, 'We absolutely *loved* you, you are just too boyish for this show right now. Come back to us in a year's time.' So I went to get a coffee, and this man, who I recognised but couldn't make out who he was, grabbed my arm and said, 'What are you doing today at five o'clock? Can you come to an audition?' There was a famous TV show that was set in Saint-Tropez at that time called *Sous le Soleil* – 'Under the Sun'. I went to the audition and suddenly recognised some of the actors there. I auditioned and they said, 'We want to offer you the job.' I was like, *what job?* 'It's for *Sous le Soleil*, but we need your answer today.' I was gobsmacked. This was 7 September 2001 and later that day, a friend of mine, a stylist, called me to say she was moving to Italy. That triggered something in me. I'd already lived in France and was ready for a new adventure – to move forward and discover what was out there for me. And I wanted to focus on dancing. I immediately said to her, 'I'm coming with you.' She replied, 'Are you stupid? You just got this massive job!' I told her I didn't care, I was already in France and wanted to go somewhere else. So I packed up all my stuff back in Belgium and drove my Citroën for nine hours from Brussels to Italy. I remember that day so clearly – it was the 11th of September and I heard the breaking news on the radio about the World Trade Center in New York. I was shaking as I drove that little car, wondering if I had made the right decision, with so many things stirring in my mind.

I arrived in Bergamo and lived there for four months, dancing in clubs. I started dancing for pop stars and going to auditions, but couldn't speak Italian. Italy isn't like London or LA, where you have agencies – people would just see you dance on a platform and if they liked the look of you and how you moved, you might be hired to dance for a new artist. It was very hard work and I wasn't making huge money. I couldn't work in a restaurant or café because I was dancing every evening, trying to make €100 a night, and during the day, I'd be so tired after not sleeping. My daily life in Italy was 5 p.m. starts and 5 a.m. finishes. And I was feeling there was something missing.

Then in November, I saw Geri Halliwell's video for 'It's Raining Men' with all these amazing dancers and I suddenly thought, *that is what I want to do.* That same year saw the release of the videos for Kylie Minogue's 'Can't Get You Out of My Head' and 'I'm a Slave 4 U' by Britney Spears. Back to back, MTV was showing these videos, and I just thought, *I want to do something better with my life.* When I told people I wanted to dance in music videos, they laughed.

Then one of my friends, who was a photographer from Belgium and living in Italy, decided to move to the UK. I told her, 'I'm coming with you.' So once again, I was on the move, and my next life was about to begin. I called my stylist friend who I'd followed to Italy and was renting a place with and she said, 'You're moving to the UK, aren't you?' I said, 'How did you know?' She said, 'Arthur, you can never stand still, you're always moving forward. Don't worry, go!'

I packed up in two hours, went back to Belgium, sold my car, and saw my family before leaving for the UK. I started to panic, thinking, I don't speak English and here I am moving to London. My friends in Belgium, who had gone to London and come back, thought I was crazy. They were better dancers than I was and were trained in ballet, contemporary or jazz. I had no formal training. They said, 'Arthur, the dancers in London are trained. You'll be eaten alive.' But others supported my decision. My stepdad Paul loved to travel and said I should follow my dreams, and my friend Julia, a make-up artist, said, 'What's the worst that can happen?'

It didn't matter what people said to me anyway, I knew this was what I needed to do. I had to let my heart decide.

Self-doubt isn't really something that happens to me. That said, before my father's death in 1996, it was a different story. But now, I was a changed man, and nothing was going to get in the way of me reaching my goals. If it didn't work out, so what?

My friend and I took the Eurostar from Brussels to London at the start of February 2002. We arrived at Waterloo station and I thought, *what now?* Neither of us spoke English, my friend had a massive camera with her, and we didn't know where to go or what to do next. We had a friend, Juliet, who worked for Eurostar in Waterloo station, so we called her and she invited us to come and stay with her in Richmond. We took the train there and walked for what seemed like forever to the house Juliet was renting. My feet were killing me. When we finally arrived, Juliet made a pot of tea and we sat down together. It was my first taste of tea with milk. Juliet said, 'Right, what is the plan?' I was thinking, *I'm now in London; where do I start?* There was no social media in those days. Instead, there was a newspaper called *The Stage*. And the one place I knew about was Pineapple Dance Studios in Covent Garden. I got an old-fashioned map out and the next day I went into the studio and the receptionist's face looked as though she were thinking, what are you doing here? I started speaking very broken English and she said, 'Wait there.' She came back with what turned out to be my godsend, Martin Matthias, who was a choreographer and dance teacher from Paris. He spoke French to me and I was so relieved. He told me to follow him downstairs and he put me in his class. I had nothing suitable to wear and he just said, 'Take off your shoes, go barefoot, and roll up your trousers.' So I did. I couldn't dance jazz, I'd never been trained, but I just went for it. We finished the class and went out for a drink and he asked me what I was doing there. I told him, 'I just arrived yesterday, I'm lost, I don't know what to do, but I want to be a dancer.' He asked if I was trained and I said no. He said, 'Arthur, the people who are here have been training for years. They're like dogs with bones.' And I said, 'I'm a dog with a bone, just without training.' He laughed and said, 'Okay, but you can't just work like this, you have to get an agent. I will help you.' We exchanged numbers and he assured me he'd support me in any way he could.

I went back to Juliet's and told the girls about my day and they couldn't believe it. A couple of days later,

I spotted an ad in *The Stage* calling for dancers for an agency called Scot Baker. I went to the audition in Dance Attic and all around me were well-groomed professional dancers dressed in black and there I was, this street boy standing there. The choreographer I was auditioning for was Kim Gavin, one of the biggest artistic directors in the world, and Gary Lloyd was the assistant choreographer. I was like, what am I *doing* here? I auditioned alongside what felt like a thousand other guys. They'd cut some people from my group, then some more and next thing I knew there were just ten of us and they pointed and said, 'You, you, you … the rest of you may go.' I didn't know what I was auditioning for, but they kept me. There were about twenty of us left from all the groups and they began talking and said to me, 'Can you sing? *Chanter?*' I mean, I *can* … Only a couple of months previously, I had to sing the song 'Belle' from *Notre Dame de Paris* for that audition so I said I could sing that. They laughed and said I could stay. I started singing and then they said, 'Can you tap?' I was like, *no* … 'Don't worry …' They started counting. They could only take five boys and they selected me. I said, 'Can I just ask what this is for?' They were like, 'You just got signed to one of the biggest agencies in the United Kingdom.'

Scot Baker was run by a woman named Lucy, who was so glamorous and sophisticated. Everybody knew her. I called Martin and told him the news. The next day, there was another audition in Dance Attic, and I just rocked up. They needed two boys for a three-month gig dancing in the evening shows at Potters resort in Great Yarmouth. I got the job along with another guy and they said because I couldn't speak English, I'd only dance and wouldn't need to work reception or anything like that. I rang Martin again, excited, and he said, 'You're not taking that job. That's not what you came here to do – you came here to dance with pop stars.' I'm like, 'But it's a job and they're paying me money to dance!' At the time, I was living in a council flat in Elephant and Castle with another guy who was working in a hotel. The job at Potters was going to pay around £300 per week but I could live there rent-free in a caravan on the premises, so I could rent out my room in London. So I said to Martin, 'Let me do this for three months and see what happens.' It ended up being a good decision because that's where I started to learn English. All I did that summer was dance and speak English.

One day, I was sitting in my caravan with my friend Michelle and the television show *Stars in Their Eyes* came on. I said, 'That's what I need to do.' Michelle said, 'Forget it, Arthur, we've all tried. Nobody ever gets that job.' In August, I finished my job at Potters and moved back to London and Scot Baker thankfully took me on. Lucy contacted me to say she had this massive audition coming up for Michele Thorne. 'She's a big choreographer. I submitted your picture and they loved it. You should go.' I asked what it was for and she said *Stars in Their Eyes*. I'd just been at the auditions for that show the day before – they were casting for four days and there were massive queues to get in. I auditioned but didn't get it, so I explained that to Lucy. She said, 'Arthur, listen to me now … you are going to this recall. You're perfect for this.' I felt like a fool going back there. I had just coloured my hair all black. They were cutting everybody. They wanted only one boy, and I got the job. My first season of *Stars in Their Eyes* with Matthew Kelly was to start shooting in September 2002 for three months. When they offered me the job, I said, 'I auditioned for you yesterday, why didn't I get it then?' They said, 'We loved you, but you had that hair colour and in this business, we don't have time to keep changing your look. We need a blank canvas.' That's when I first learned the importance of how I presented myself.

I started working on the show and because I wasn't technically trained, Michele Thorne always put me in the back. She was very tough. One day I said to her, 'Why are you always putting me in the back?' She said, 'Arthur, I love you, but you are not technical.' I replied, 'So why did you employ me?' She said, 'Because you're amazing. The power you have in your dancing – you can't teach that.' I loved working on that show and after that, my career began to take off. Step by step, I was getting discovered by people in the industry.

*****

I have the words 'Everything happens for a reason' tattooed on my right calf. I got it done near Dublin's Temple Bar, funnily enough, in 2007, but it's a belief I've always held.

If things are meant for you, they will happen. At the same time, life won't just come to you – you have to work hard, you have to go out and get it, but I really do believe you can make something happen if you really want it badly enough.

Kim Gavin and Gary Lloyd, who I first auditioned for, got in contact with me saying they were casting dancers for *Blue Peter*. The day we were shooting, I kept saying my shoes were slipping on the floor and nobody paid any attention. As I was dancing to Bananarama's 'Venus', I jumped down from the stage to the lower floor and slipped and my knee went. They were filming with a zoom camera and when the camera came towards me as I landed, it hit my face. I was on the floor screaming. Then I had these flashes and everything was blurry. People were screaming, 'What's happened?' My knee was literally gone. I thought, *this is it, I'm done, my career is over.*

Gary said to me, 'Do you have some money? If you go to the NHS, you might never dance again. We know someone in The Harley Street Clinic – he's very expensive but he looks after the top dancers – we all go there.' I didn't know how much it would cost but I knew I had to try it. It was so expensive. My ligaments were completely gone. I was determined to finish the shoot so I returned three days later with a brace on my knee. I was in so much pain. I decided then to take a break from dancing for six months to heal. I didn't know what the future would hold at that point.

Kim Gavin and Gary Lloyd rang me again in November and asked if I would do the Royal Variety Performance the following month. I didn't know what the Royal Variety was and I said I couldn't do it because of my injury. They said no problem, rest. I hung up the phone and my friend asked what the phone call was about. When I told her, she explained that the Royal Variety was *the* most prestigious show in the UK. I got them back on the phone and said I'd do it. I couldn't pass up an opportunity like that. I was the Royal Variety dancer, performing with Will Young, Anastacia, Liberty X, Gareth Gates and other artists. It was so difficult, I was suffering in silence the whole time, but because Kim and Gary knew about my injury – and how hungry I was – if there was a move I couldn't do, they made allowances for that. And I received my certificate from the Queen at the end of it. My feeling at the time was that I couldn't give up, I needed to succeed. Looking back now, though, I wouldn't advise other dancers to put themselves at risk dancing through injuries like I did.

I continued with the treatments in Harley Street but was told my knee would never fully recover. An operation was possible but it would result in one of my legs being shorter than the other, and as a dancer, that wasn't a real option for me.

*****

On 27 December 2002, I went to a club with a guy I had been seeing for a few weeks. It was a Friday and we broke up that night. Left on my own, I was ready to go home, but then Deborah Cox's 'Absolutely Not' started playing – that song was huge, so I decided to stay. I was dancing on my own, not looking to find anyone, just having fun. And that's when I first saw him – Brian Dowling was on the other side of the room, like a mirage. He was so handsome, so my type, and he was coming towards me wearing a Burberry shirt. When he spoke to me, I tried to explain that I spoke very little English and he walked away. I was like, that's okay, I'm fine – I don't get upset by such things. And I started eyeing up this blond guy who looked like an Abercrombie & Fitch model. It turned out to be Brian's best friend's brother, who was actually straight. I didn't realise the two of them were together in the same group. Then Brian started talking to him and his other friends and suddenly he was standing in front of me. He then started talking to me again and we began flirting. Next thing I knew people were taking pictures with their cameras. I didn't know what was going on or why they would be taking our photos. Brian asked me what I did for a living and I told him I was a dancer. He was like, 'Yeah right, of course you are. One of those go-go dancers, right?' I'm like, 'No, I'm a professional dancer.'

I asked what he did and he lied and said he worked in PR. I didn't know what that was. I think he thought I would recognise him, but I hadn't a clue who he was – I didn't watch *Big Brother* and knew nothing about the show. I just thought he was cute, with those greenish-blue eyes of his. We left the club together and kissed. We started dating and having fun, and I told Brian that I was doing rehearsals – I was dancing for Zoe Birkett from *Pop Idol*, there were four girls and two boys and I was one of them.

A week later, I was doing *CD:UK* with Zoe, and I was standing in the studio canteen and Brian walked by with Tess Daly. I called to him and he just blanked me, totally ignored me and carried on. I turned to the woman I was talking with in the canteen and said, 'That's the guy I've been seeing. Why is he here?' She replied, 'You've been dating Brian Dowling?' She laughed and didn't believe me because Brian was so famous at the time, but I still didn't know who he was.

So next thing, I'm on stage dancing and I look over at Brian and Tess and I know he sees me. The following day we went out for coffee and I asked him what he was doing there. He explained he was actually a TV presenter. And I'm like, *oh, that's nice.* I think he expected me to be starstruck or something, but I wasn't fazed. I liked the guy I met in the club. He was funny, he made me laugh. I wasn't looking to date a celebrity. I just wanted to get to know him.

From then on, things were a little awkward. We decided to keep our relationship private. I didn't want people to know I was dating this famous person – I never wanted to be famous myself, so the celebrity thing didn't matter to me. People would flirt with him in clubs, which didn't bother me because I'm quite secure – there is no point in jealousy. And I wanted to make my own way in the world, not become a success because of who I was with.

We were falling in love but at the same time, I didn't feel Brian was treating me the way I deserved to be treated. I wasn't happy being ignored or pushed to the side. He'd never say he had a boyfriend because of his job. So we were on and off, on and off … for years.

Meanwhile, my career was really taking off. I auditioned for choreographer Priscilla Samuels – who famously worked with the Spice Girls – to dance with Liberty X, and I got the job. She said to me, 'When I saw you dancing, the energy you gave in that room, I knew you were hungry.' Priscilla was the best human to work with. She is an incredible choreographer and was so good to me. She believed in me. I ended up touring with Liberty X on private jets while they were promoting their single 'Being Nobody'.

I was doing tour after tour. I was booked to do the first-ever *Pop Idol* tour in Germany. I was living my dream. Only, my family weren't there to see it and all that really mattered to me was making *them* proud. Also, I was having so much success at that time that sadly, I was making a few enemies too, because I was getting the jobs they weren't, and I was the foreigner who wasn't formally trained. Some people tried to put me down, saying I couldn't really dance, but I got the jobs because I worked hard, gave every audition my all, had energy and on top of all of that, I really networked. I took advantage of every opportunity I had to talk with people and ask how I might get to work with a certain choreographer or artist. That's what I had to do – there was no social media back then, it was all word of mouth. My goal was to work with artists like Geri Halliwell and Kylie Minogue, and I remained focused on that. Then one day, a Spanish guy I knew said he would get me the email address for a very famous Italian choreographer named Luca Tommassini and advised me to send my stuff to him. So I sent the email and ended up getting a job working with Geri Halliwell. The first gig was in the London nightclub G-A-Y, where the biggest pop stars would perform. I was half-naked on stage and it was a big performance for Geri. It was surreal – a real pinch-me moment. Everything I had done up until this point was leading to this. And things just kept getting better and better. People were recognising me. I was one of the first people to dance on *The X Factor*. I was taking the good and leaving the bad.

Before I got to London, I used to spend every New Year's Eve in a different location. So as we got ready to ring in 2003, I stood on my own in the middle of the crowd in Piccadilly Circus, just sucking in all the energy and thinking to myself, *I am going to make everything happen.*

I later had this massive audition for the 2004 film *Beyond the Sea*, a biopic about the singer Bobby Darin starring Kevin Spacey (though I didn't know who Kevin Spacey was at the time). They were looking for stage boys. The choreographer Rob Marshall was there and I remember thinking, this is going to be so tough for me, I'm not technically trained, I don't know what I'm going to do. We did the routine, it was very jazzy, very Broadway, and the choreographer stopped us. I was always in the back, and he pointed and beckoned me to come forward and I'm thinking, what's going to happen? I'm going to be embarrassed, he's just going to show how ridiculous I

am. And he just said, 'Dance!' So I just went for it – *Bam!
Bam! Bam!* He stopped the music and said, 'This is what
I'm looking for!' I got hired on the spot.

There were times in my career when I wouldn't get the
job I wanted – even times when someone would stab me
in the back – but I never allowed myself to get upset. I
would never let anything bring me down. I'd just shake it
off and say, 'It's just an audition, just a job.' There's no need
to get upset about these things. It's not worth it. In the
greater scheme of things, none of that matters. And I'm a
helper – all my life, I've pushed others. I sometimes prefer
watching my friends succeed. Throughout my dancing
career, I never had to work a day job in a shop or restaurant. There were times when I didn't have much money
and worried about how I'd pay my rent, but I never had to
find other work to support my dancing career. Something
always came up and I was able to work solely as a professional dancer. So I was very lucky. I was also the biggest
male dancer in size. All the other boys were skinny and
petite – a size 30. I was tall and chunky – a size 34 or
36. I remember one time I was wearing a topless costume
and the choreographer thought I might need to go on a

diet, just to be sure I looked alright on stage. Thank God I wasn't insecure; none of that really affected me.

Kylie Minogue kept cropping up throughout my career. In 2004, a friend of mine called to tell me about an audition to dance for Kylie and I nearly dropped the phone. She was doing these small concerts in France, Spain and Italy. It was incredible, I loved every single minute of that job. Years later, I got called to workshop with the choreographer on the KylieX2008 tour.

While all of this was happening for me, Brian and I were on again and off again because he wasn't treating me the way I wanted to be treated. But in 2005 we were back together, and he gave me a dollar bill for my 25th birthday, saying we were going on a trip to New York. I was ecstatic; that city was always on my wish list. But it turned out to be the worst trip of my life. Brian spent most of the time with his friends. Anything I suggested we do, he said no. So I went off on my own and that's when I met one of my all-time greatest friends, Terry. He was a businessman from Memphis and I met him while sitting alone in a café. He was dressed in a suit and asked if I would pass him the newspaper and we got to talking. If I hadn't gone out on my own that day, I never would have met this wonderful person.

Brian and I came home from that trip and it was the beginning of the end of our relationship. I had already moved out and was living with a friend and in February 2006, I was on a job in Manchester and met this dancer, another Irish man, who was flirting with me and giving me the kind of attention Brian never did. I came home after that job in March and broke up with Brian for the final time saying, 'I can't do this anymore.' Brian wasn't making an effort and I was fed up, but I could tell I had truly broken his heart. We remained friends for the next five years and in that time, the odd friend would say to me, 'You should get back with Brian.' But I needed to be with someone who would treat me right, and I didn't think Brian could do that. And I *had* moved on. I dated that other Irish guy for a year and a half, I was on tour a lot, meeting so many people. I felt like the king of the world. And for five years, Brian wanted me back, but I was adamant I was not going back to him.

*****

By 2010, I got to a point where I knew I was going to stop dancing. I got a call about a video for Kylie Minogue's new song, 'Get Outta My Way'. They were like, 'We know you, you're booked.' I didn't have to audition, I just got the job. All the dancers were platinum blond in that video, including me, and I loved doing it. But by that stage, I was thinking, what's next?

In all my years as a dancer, I was the only one with facial hair – I always had stubble or a beard – and that year, I was working on *The X Factor Live Show*. One Direction was singing 'Kids in America' and I was one of the dancers in that performance, and I remember Simon Cowell said all the dancers needed to shave to make us all look younger. I didn't want to shave off my beard. My facial hair was a part of me that I wasn't willing to let go of so easily. To change my look for one performance, only to have to grow it back later, wasn't worth the effort, especially as I had come to the decision to stop dancing. It just felt like the time had come to wrap up that chapter in my career. I didn't want to be a 30-year-old dancer, competing with younger people. My heart was no longer in it. I was grateful to be able to dance full-time for ten years but it was simply time to move on.

At the end of 2010, I did my last Royal Variety Performance with Take That, working again with Kim Gavin. Take That were performing 'The Flood' and it was the first performance to feature Robbie Williams since he re-joined the band. There were about a hundred dancers on stage. We were basically naked, wearing a G-string that only covered our genitalia. When my agent told me about the job, I thought, *I'm not doing that!* Then I just figured, *I'll be in the back, it'll be fine.* But I was brought to the very front of the stage – I was right in front of the camera with my big Armenian nose, you couldn't miss me. I was retiring as a dancer with my naked body on UK national TV, in front of the Queen. There were younger dancers behind me with my bare ass in front of them. It was so weird, but I did it. I had the most epic career as a dancer from 2000 to 2010 and this was a fantastic way to end that chapter of my life.

*****

Two years earlier, I was at a wrap party with Will Young and met Sojin Lee, who worked with 19 Entertainment – the agency behind *Pop Idol* and the Spice Girls. I didn't know who she was but we got to talking. After a while, she asked if I would mind driving her friends to a club. Her friends ended up being James Corden, Dominic Cooper and Amanda Seyfried. Dominic and Amanda were in the back of my car and James was in the passenger seat. In November 2010, I got a phone call from Sojin. She remembered me saying to her that night that I wanted to get into choreography and told me she was working on a new project for Fashionair – Christian Louboutin was launching his first men's shoe and the idea was to have him dance like Fred Astaire in a video wearing the shoes. It would be the first time he'd ever danced so they were looking for a choreographer who could work with him. I didn't know who Christian Louboutin was, but I just pitched myself for the job – we'd film it in Paris, in black and white, there would be two women dancing with him … the whole shebang. Two hours after I met with them, I got a call from Sojin telling me I got the job. I taught Christian Louboutin to dance, we had fun and after we filmed the video, he sent me a pair of the new shoes – he only did that for Pharrell Williams, Mika and me. He said, 'If it wasn't for Arthur, I would never have been able to dance.'

Before I took that job, I planned on returning to hairdressing. I bought all the gear and everything. I would never have called myself a choreographer. Then, that video went viral, so I thought, *I can do this*. I put my hairdressing kit aside and started working on these big corporate jobs and events, working with massive brands that paid a lot of money. Choreography had now become a business for me. I was doing all the Puma launches, working with Selena Gomez, Cara Delevingne, Rihanna … It was surreal but everything was just coming my way naturally. And I was enjoying the ride.

The other side of it, though, was that while I was getting loads of choreography work, I was also losing friends because I'd become a threat. When I was a dancer, I kept my mouth shut and just did the work. As a creative choreographer, I'd found my voice and was using it. I remember someone was suggesting I assist another choreographer and my American friend Terry, who's always been a huge support to me said, 'Why are you asking Arthur to assist him? He could have his own career.' And that's when it clicked … people didn't want me to succeed. I lost so many friends, but I did nothing wrong. I just stepped into choreography. I wasn't out to take anyone else's job – I'm not that person. I just wanted to work and do the best job I could. Since I started doing choreography, my career took me from one job to the next. People came to me looking for me to work with them, and I became so busy I had to turn jobs down. I was creating a new life for myself. That's when I first made the decision to go to America and I started looking into how I could get a visa.

*****

A year later, in July 2011, Brian and I met up for dinner. We were both single and he was handsome and looking very sleek. Something was different about him. When I got home, I texted him, suggesting we do it again soon. We met up a couple more times and then one day I said to him, 'Can I kiss you?' And it was like we were transported back to 2002. It felt amazing all over again, but it also felt new. I think in that time apart, Brian needed to learn to appreciate me and I needed to know whether he truly loved me. For the next few months, we were dating but didn't tell anyone because we knew our friends would think we were just going back down the same path and would end up hurting each other again. We needed to see where this was going without people trying to talk us out of it or worrying about us or being excited that we were back together only for us to break up again and upset everyone. When we finally told everyone at Halloween, some people were confused and others were like, 'Listen, you two have such a history, do whatever you have to do.' But we both knew that this was finally the right time for us.

Once we were back together, Brian made it clear he wanted us to get married. Marriage wasn't something I needed at the time – I always wanted a family, but I didn't necessarily want to get married. Since it was so important to Brian, I knew I was going to have to be the one who asked. For the next three years, Brian waited patiently, dropping hints from time to time, but the time was never right for me – I was choreographing, travelling, and doing lots of different jobs. And Brian was hosting *Big Brother* and after that ended, he was in a dark place.

We went to our friend Sojin Lee's wedding in 2014, and the designer Roland Mouret was there. He was telling me how happy he was with his husband James Webster and he said to me, 'What are you waiting for?'

We went on holiday in 2014 to the Dominican Republic. We were staying in the Hard Rock Hotel – it was very rock 'n' roll. I knew it was time to ask him, but nobody else knew – I didn't tell anyone what I was planning.

The only problem was, I'm very adventurous and Brian is not. So I suggested we go on a helicopter ride and he said no, so I had to cancel that. I said, 'Let's go to a private beach?' He said, 'I don't want to go to a beach on our own!' Everything I suggested, he didn't want to do. I remember this poor woman who arranged everything for me, she would see me approaching and say, 'Don't tell me we're changing it again!' We changed plans four times! But Brian didn't know what was going on. Finally, it was 30 July, we had two days left on our holiday and we were coming back from the beach sunburned. Brian was covered in mosquito bites. I thought, *to hell with it*. I ran back to the room and threw some rose petals on the bed along with this tacky swan. I had my dad's ring and put it on a drumstick (because I've always loved the drums) and placed a card down on the bed that said, 'Marry me.' We walked into the room together, and Brian said, 'What is that? The hotel staff must have thought we just got married!' I told him, 'Look at the card!' He read it and turned around to me and I said, 'Will you marry me?' We both started crying. It was far from glamorous but it didn't matter. We were engaged and happy. We'd buy our rings later together – my dad's ring was just for the proposal. It was the best moment and we couldn't wait to start our lives together.

PART TWO

<u>5</u>

BRIAN AND ARTHUR:

Beginning our new life together

We returned home from that holiday ready to start our lives together and began planning our wedding as soon as we got back. We visited potential venues all through that September and made an agreement that after each visit we'd leave the premises and go, 'On the count of three – one, two, three …' and simultaneously cast our vote as to whether that place was a goer. Our friends Pippa O'Connor and Brian Ormond held their wedding in Powerscourt in County Wicklow so we went to check it out. We'd forgotten how spectacular it was, and the moment we walked out of our meeting with the hotel we went, 'One, two, three … Yes!' We'd found our wedding venue.

A lot of people probably assumed we were waiting for the marriage equality referendum to go through before we got married in Ireland, but it was just a coincidence that the Marriage Equality Act passed on 22 May 2015 and we were married two months later on 30 July, exactly one year after we got engaged. We had in fact been planning our nuptials for many months and on that beautiful summer's day, around 200 of our closest friends and family gathered together wrapped in the embrace of the Wicklow Mountains to celebrate our union. We were so grateful for their love and support.

*****

BRIAN

I'm not going to lie – I played a bit of the bride role in the lead-up to our wedding, probably worrying more about how I was going to look while Arthur – being the creative director that he is – took charge and was running around organising every last detail to be sure the celebration went beautifully. My sister Paula's wedding was also taking place that July, so she was raging that I tried to steal her thunder. And while we were making arrangements for our big day, Ireland was deciding whether or not we should even be allowed to marry.

My Catholic mother had great faith and we always went to Mass as a family until we reached a certain age – when we left secondary school and were no longer required to go to church if we didn't want to, but Mum still went. I think it was around the time of the marriage equality referendum, when people were putting up posters saying, 'Vote no', that she stopped going. Writing this book in 2023, it seems absolutely ridiculous to me that only eight years ago in this country, complete strangers had the power to affect how I could live my life. All around us, there were people holding up signs encouraging others to vote against marriage equality, and my mum was mortified when all that was happening. I remember her saying in the car, 'Who are these people to be putting up signs? Don't let anyone stop you, son.'

Mum walked me down the aisle on our wedding day. She was so nervous. My mother was never a glamour puss, she never had time to focus on her appearance.

We went shopping for her dress in Newbridge and I told her I could have a private room organised. She was like, 'I don't need a private room.' She hated attention. And the day of my wedding was no different. I had all my friends there, like Vernon Kay and Tess Daly, and Mum told me she didn't want to meet anyone famous. Of course, whether they were famous or not, our guests wanted to meet my mum, but I think the attention just made her uncomfortable. She couldn't wait for it to be over so she could go home, back to normality, to cook the dinner and look after her grandchildren.

And as my wedding day approached, I became more and more obsessed with losing weight. I didn't eat much of anything for probably five days beforehand. I did juices, worked out, and saw a dietitian and a personal trainer … I was hellbent on being the thinnest I could be and lost nearly five stone, and because I exercised so much, it was all muscle. I remember Tess saying to me she thought I looked too thin. After the wedding was over, I had to actually retrain myself to eat normally again. I don't say that lightly and actually feel slightly embarrassed admitting that now, but it's the truth. A couple of days after the wedding, I had a craving for chips with taco sauce and a quarter pounder and once I had it in front of me, I couldn't eat it. I felt nauseous. I couldn't maintain the level I'd got to: it wasn't normal. And while I'm happy that I looked my best for my wedding photos, there are pictures of me taken at other times where I look obese because I've always had an issue with food, either binging or starving myself. I think people associate people who are not eating with those who are stick-thin, that you have to look a certain way to have an eating issue. I worked my ass off that year. Was it the right thing to do? No, but I wanted to look my absolute fittest and I think anyone in that situation knows what that feels like. Thankfully, when it comes to stuff like that now, I'm way more in check with myself. There are still times when I'd binge or eat less, but I'm way healthier about it now than I was.

I feel like the wedding was more for me than it was for Arthur. I wanted the traditional wedding, for it to be as heterosexual as possible. That might sound odd, but like my mother, I'm very old-fashioned in that respect. People would keep referring to it as a 'gay wedding' and I'd say, 'It's not a gay wedding – it's *our* wedding.' I was also adamant at the time that it would be a real show. I wanted it to look like one of the weddings you'd see in a celebrity magazine. That said, when publications approached us offering to run our wedding photos, we declined because we wanted our guests to be able to just relax and enjoy the day and take their own photographs if they wanted to.

When the day finally arrived, it was full-on. I had just two glasses of champagne – Arthur doesn't drink and he'd normally be with me when I'm tipsy and on this occasion, I wanted us both to enjoy our day together, so I decided I wouldn't drink any more than that. We both wore Tom Ford and Simon was my best man. I remember we considered having this expensive red carpet and Arthur initially said no and then on the day, it was there to welcome us. Arthur had it arranged as he wanted everything to be perfect for me. We had this fake wall that dropped to reveal the bar and dancefloor and we had our first dance to RyanDan's 'Like the Sun'. I wanted our song to be something no one had heard before. Arthur was giving out because I kept standing on his feet. And as we danced, I looked around at all our guests standing together, our friends and family who were so happy we'd finally gotten here, and it was an amazing moment.

As magical as everything was, I do feel it was just a little too big and I was so nervous hoping everything would go smoothly and everyone else was looked after that I don't think I enjoyed the day as much as I should have. The next day, though, was brilliant. We had a barbecue on the roof of the hotel and had the whole top floor and I drank a bottle of champagne while having a blow-dry. And I loved wearing my wedding rings – I was obsessed with them. That day felt so much more laid back. Mum was much more relaxed and felt more like herself, wearing trousers instead of a dress.

When we look at the pictures and see the people who were at our top table, only a few of those people are still in our lives, which is quite sad, but life happens. Things are said and there's always three sides to any story – my side, their side and the truth. I never say never. I shared my wedding and parts of my life with these people and have a lot of respect for each of them. When I was broken-hearted or faced any struggles, they were there for me then. It's just unfortunate they're no longer in my life now.

After we were married, I chose to take Arthur's surname. I wanted whatever family we might be blessed with to one day have the name Dowling Gourounlian.

*****

ARTHUR

I had avoided contact with my family ever since I came out to my mother because I didn't want to have to lie to anyone about who I was, and who I chose to spend my life with. I think some of my family members must have realised I was gay over the years – I took part in the Eurovision Song Contest in 2006 dancing with the entry for Turkey and coincidentally, that just so happened to be the first year Armenia participated in Eurovision so if anyone saw me on television, they probably could have guessed. My mother was so worried at the time.

By 2015, I was long done pretending and my mother had no patience for any family member that didn't accept me for who I was. And after Brian and I announced our engagement and news of our wedding went viral – in

Ireland, the UK, America, even Belgium and Armenia –
any suspicions my relatives may have had about my sexuality were well and truly confirmed.

Suddenly, I was getting calls from practically everyone in my family. I received death threats. An aunt of mine rang my mother, shouting down the phone at her. I went crazy and said to my aunt, 'Don't you dare ever speak to me again. Delete my number.' To this day, I don't speak to any of my extended family bar two or three cousins. My dad's brother, the uncle living in Belgium, thought my being gay was disgusting so I no longer speak to him either. Once everybody knew, I decided to focus my energy on living my life to the fullest. And my mother has been my biggest supporter. She told all of my relatives, one by one, never to contact me again.

When Brian and I got married, my mum was crying and Brian joked that her tears meant she mustn't want us to get married, and I told him that actually, it was because she was so happy. She never dreamed I'd have a beautiful wedding and marry the love of my life. I'd finally found the happiness she wanted so much for me.

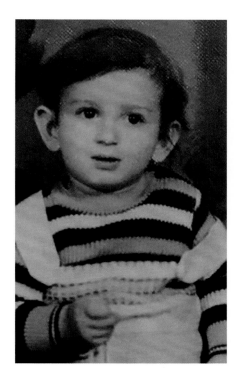

ARTHUR: Me, age two. I was very shy, believe it or not!

BRIAN: Here is baby Brian. This was taken in our sitting room. I presume it was summer, as I'm wearing shorts. I'm no more than two years old. My mum told me I actually had ringworm when this pic was taken. How lovely! Arthur has the original copy of this, as he loves the picture so much.

ARTHUR: A Gourounlian family portrait. In Armenia, it was a yearly tradition to have a family picture taken by a professional photographer. Here I am with my mum and dad and my gorgeous sister, Nazik.

ARTHUR: My grandmother Anahit, who is my dad's mother, used to love dressing her grandkids up and making us pose for a photographer. I adore this picture. It's called FASHION, people!

BRIAN: This was my sister Aoife's Holy Communion in 1996. Pictured with me are my mum, dad and my sisters – Michelle, Valerie, Tara and, of course, Aoife. I actually did my mum's hair for this, because around that time I wanted to be a hairdresser.

BRIAN: Okay, Aoife will hate me for including this picture. I can't tell you when this picture was taken, but even back then we were super close.

BRIAN: Pictures like this will always mean so much to me. Especially as they include Mum. This was the night I was crowned the winner of *Big Brother* back in 2001. To be honest, most of that night is still a bit of a blur. (© PA Images/Alamy Stock Photo)

ARTHUR: This is Cheryl and me on the Girls Aloud Out of Control tour in 2009. I spent four years of my dancing career with the girls. Those years were so magical. This tour will always mean a lot to me, as it was my last tour as a dancer.

BRIAN: In my wildest dreams, I never would have thought it was possible to win *Big Brother* twice. But it happened. This is me leaving the *Ultimate Big Brother* house as the champion back in September 2010. I cannot believe I'm still the only person to have won *Big Brother UK* twice. (© PA Images/Alamy Stock Photo)

ARTHUR: There are dreams you hope to accomplish, and you do everything in your power to make them happen. Despite being a foreigner whose first language wasn't English, an incredible dream really came true: appearing on *Dancing with the Stars*, the biggest live television show in Ireland. I am still pinching myself. (© KOBPIX)

On a weekend in Ireland in January 2004, spending time with our friends. We were so young back then and really had no idea what we were doing.

ARTHUR: Brian surprised me and my friends with lunch in Soho to celebrate my twenty-third birthday. Can we just talk about his flip phone? He was obsessed with it!

Our wedding day
on 30 July 2015.
Memories for life.

BRIAN: My mum was never one for GLAMOUR, so I love this pic of her and my dad on my wedding day. She was so nervous walking me down the aisle.

BRIAN: This was taken at a gathering we had for my podcast, *Death Becomes Him.* We invited all the guests from each episode. Here I am with all of my sisters: (from left to right) Michelle, Tracey, Aoife, Paula, Valerie and Tara. This was November 2021. We had spent most of that year trying to get pregnant. Amazingly, a few weeks later we did.

BRIAN: Our baby shower on the rooftop of The Marker Hotel in August 2022. It was the hottest day of the year. We celebrated with all our family and friends. We had told no one that we were having a baby girl, so the theme was blue and pink. The shirt I wore that day is so important to me that I decided to wear it for the book cover.

I September 2022: the day that changed our lives. Aoife was incredibly brave that day. This pic was taken minutes before she went into theatre.

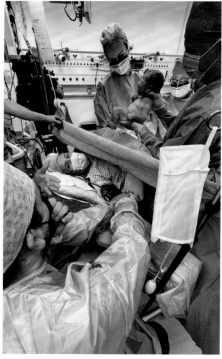

Here we are like two doctors from *Grey's Anatomy*. Ready to meet our baby girl!

This photo says it all. Meeting Blake Maria Rose for the very first time.

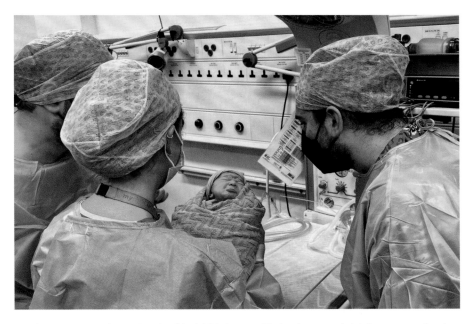

At this point, neither of us had held Blake yet. To be honest, I think we were both in shock.

Our very first picture as a family of three.

Our beautiful daughter, Blake Maria Rose, born 1 September 2022 at 14.54, weighing 7lb 4oz.

2 September 2022: Blake's first day at home with Daddy and Papa. From day one she was such a good sleeper.

Blake's christening on 10 December 2022. It was important to us to have it on this day, as it was also Brian's mum Rosie's birthday.

Our very first Christmas with Blake. This was the night of *The Late Late Toy Show*. We can confirm that Blake missed all of it, but Daddy and Papa enjoyed every minute.

Tati, aka Grandma Maria. This picture was taken in January 2023 on the day Tati flew back to France. She had arrived in October 2022 and we had the best three months with her.

BRIAN: Marseille Airport in May 2023. This was our first-ever holiday with Blake and her first time on a plane. We flew to the south of France to visit Arthur's family. Due to work, I flew back ahead of Arthur and Blake. I was so emotional leaving them.

Our beautiful ray of sunshine.

I will never forget the first time my mum met Brian's mum, Rosie. It was just before our wedding. Rosie and Brian's sister Tara came to see us, my mum was there and we all had afternoon tea together. Brian and I wondered how the two of them would communicate, as my mum spoke French and Rosie spoke English. But the two of them got on so well and it just went to prove that love will always find a way. They were both laughing and it was such a beautiful moment to see these two wonderful women talking to one another.

Our wedding was like a mirage to me if I'm honest. It went by so fast and because I'm such a control freak, even though we had a wedding planner, I organised so many details myself. I couldn't help it. I splashed out on a chandelier to hang over our top table, just to surprise Brian. It was worth it, too, just to see his face when we walked into the room. He loved it. But I was running around sorting things out at the last minute as I wanted to make sure everybody was well looked after. It was a three-day celebration and to this day, our guests talk about how wonderful it all was. Our wedding was incredible – the most epic, beautiful day and I loved every minute of it – I just couldn't relax while it was actually happening.

Two years after we married, I reminded Brian of my intention to move to America. I had done everything I wanted to do in the UK and told him I needed to go. I don't think he ever believed I'd do it. I applied for my visa, and I will never forget that I was in the car with my mum and my sister when I got the call from my lawyers saying it had all been approved. I was going to America. It was an epic moment for me and the three of us all started crying in that car. Brian cried too when I told him. He was like, 'You've done it! Everything you say you'll do, you do!' Brian got signed to an American agent and applied for his visa and got it soon after.

I left for America in October 2017 and stayed in New York at the beginning, living with my American friend Terry for three months. I had meetings and was told by several people that for the type of work I did, I needed to be in Los Angeles. New York was Broadway, but LA was where I'd find work in commercials, films and with pop artists. So I moved to LA in February 2018. No sooner had I arrived than I got a short-term job working in

Armenia on the Eurovision entry for a few weeks. That's when Brian finally followed me to LA. I'm not sure his heart was ever fully in the idea of living in America but he made that commitment to be with me while I pursued my ambitions. The day after he arrived, he received a phone call that would cement his view on living in the US from that day forward.

6

BRIAN AND ROSIE

No amount of words on this earth can adequately describe just how much my mother has meant to me, and to every single person whose life she touched. My mother, Rosie Dowling, in case I've yet to make this clear, lived her life for her family. While other people may have been winning awards, my mother decided that her children were her seven gold medals – badges of honour she wore with great pride.

The day I flew over to LA to follow Arthur in his pursuit of the American dream, I rang my mum to tell her I had arrived safe and sound. I was staying in the home of my good friend Donal Skehan, minding his dog while he stayed in my apartment in London. The last thing Mum said to me before hanging up the phone was 'Goodnight, son'. I awoke at midnight LA time to another phone call, this time from my sister Tracey. She was distraught ... our gorgeous, inimitable mother passed away in her sleep on 21 February 2018. She was just 61. It was a case of Sudden Adult Death Syndrome – she wasn't sick – there had been no reason for me to think I would never hear my beloved mother's voice again after I ended that call the night before. I couldn't breathe, let alone believe what I was hearing. My friend Leighann, who's a cabin manager with Aer Lingus, helped me get on an urgent flight back to Ireland. I remember sitting on that plane on my own knowing my mum had passed away and thinking, *please somebody change this – don't let this be happening.* It was crippling.

When I finally arrived at the house in Rathangan and got out of the car, my legs didn't work and I fell into my sister Valerie's arms thinking, *I can't do this.* I didn't know what to do. It fills me with such anxiousness still. I felt so vulnerable and the realisation hit me that the one person who would always protect me was gone. Mum always looked out for me, from the time I came out to the time she defended me against that teacher and anyone else who ever said anything against me. And to have that person removed from my life without any notice was the cruellest thing. I remember just feeling like a child again. When I got out of that car, it felt as if that teacher had hit me again. I couldn't walk and Valerie helped me into the house, and suddenly there were all these people. I wanted to shout, 'Get out!' I sat in the kitchen and all around me were people making tea while aunts and uncles were in the sitting room with the coffin. I've never gotten over the fact that I couldn't grieve privately. I came home to a house full of visitors and never had that quiet moment alone with Mum. It made me so angry. I sat in that chair, exhausted from jetlag and completely overwhelmed with sadness. The next morning, I awoke while it was still dark and sat on a stool in my pyjamas until 3.30 a.m. My uncle Thomas – Mum's youngest brother – was there along with two of my sisters and I finally said to them, 'Okay, I'm going in to look at her.'

Before that day, I had never seen anyone who had died. My sisters, apart from Aoife, had all seen our mother warm in her bed. When I finally saw her lying in that coffin, I just saw a woman. There was a picture beside it, which looked like Mum – it showed her personality, her rosy cheeks. The woman in the coffin didn't look like my mother at all.

I just remember feeling so sad for Mum, and wanted to swap places with her. Before that moment, I'd never felt like giving up my life for anyone, but I'd have gladly jumped into that coffin and taken Mum out of it in a heartbeat … because my mother deserved to be alive. She was a saint. I looked at her in the coffin thinking, *why are you dead? What have we done to deserve this? What could we have done differently?*

Of course, the answer to that question was nothing. My mum died because that was always going to happen, and I'm just thankful she was in her bed when it did. She always told us she wanted to die in her own home. I actually discussed Mum's funeral with her before she died – it was a coincidence, we were joking when she turned 60, and I said I was going to send her to a home and she laughed and said she'd outlive me. Then I asked her what she wanted at her funeral and she said loads of fresh flowers, and she didn't want us wearing black (I wore a navy suit). She also wanted the song 'Seven Spanish Angels' played.

Mum had seven children and that's why that song was so important to her – we were her seven angels.

The last message Mum sent to us in our group chat was a picture of our grandfather's grave. It read: 'My dad would have been 100 today.' Mum had wanted to be cremated but she said to my father that day, 'Aren't grave-yards a lovely place? Because people can come and talk to the person and pay their respects.' This was the Sunday before she died. That same day she showed Tara, who still lived at home, how to make a Sunday roast. It was so odd and I often wonder if she knew what was to come.

My wonderful friend Pippa O'Connor Ormond, who lost her own mum in 2014, said to me after Mum died, 'People are going to show you who they are now. Believe them.' She was right. I learned who my true friends were after Mum died. Arthur was delayed joining me in Rathangan – he was working in Armenia when we learned of Mum's death and was on his way to Barcelona for another job and there were very few flights available, so he arrived just in time for the funeral. So Simon and Leighann both dropped everything to be there with me. I wasn't taking care of myself and nearly fainted. Simon, who's used to working with the most fabulous people as a PR, was spoon-feeding me chicken curry, and Leighann was running around making tea for everyone. They both rallied around me. Simon is like the brother I never had. That same day, he went out to a shop and came back with a giant bag of Chilli Doritos because he knew I liked them. That really broke me – it was just a bag of Doritos, but what it symbolised was that he cared so much about me. Leighann was going through a divorce at that time and was due to go on a date with our friend, Nadia Forde's uncle Filippo, the night before the funeral. Leighann was going to cancel the date and I told her she couldn't because Mum was always asking after her, wondering if she was seeing anyone, so Mum would have wanted her to go. Leighann sat beside me at the funeral and I turned to her and said, 'How was the date?' They actually hit it off and are still together – imagine if she had cancelled. That scenario provided a nice distraction for me on a day when I was so numb.

I looked around at everyone in the church and just felt so angry. I didn't want people to shake my hand, to commiserate with me, which is so ridiculous because two years later, when Covid happened and people couldn't say goodbye in this way, I realised then how lucky we were. It was a room full of love and respect, and people had our backs. But at that time I couldn't appreciate that. My sister Tara was wailing in a way I'd never heard before. They were putting Mum into the ground and I remember noticing how deep it was. Since then, I've always believed that a part of me – and each of my sisters – went in the ground with my mother. I wouldn't want it any other way because I'm not the same person I was before she died, and I think Mum deserves to have a part of all of us with her.

When it was all over, we came home and walked into the house and it felt so empty and quiet. I said to Arthur, 'Every day from here on, for the rest of my life, it's going to be so different. Every time I'm in this house, I'm just going to feel lonely.' And I always have. It's amazing, when you remove one person, what it does to a place. It just shows how powerful my mother was.

Over the coming days, I couldn't get out of bed. Maybe I was depressed or in shock. I was also exhausted – between the jetlag and grieving and dealing with the funeral arrangements and people coming to the house,

I hadn't slept. My sister Tracey came into my room and said, 'Get out of bed!' I told her to go away. I don't think I had brushed my teeth or had a shower in two days. And Tracey, who's as loud as I am, roared at me, 'Oh my God, are you actually serious? You're going to do this to us? Get a grip. What did Mum always say to us?' Our mum always believed the show must go on. Whatever happens, you paint a smile on your face. You do that for the family. And Tracey just said, 'Mum would say to you, "Get dressed, put a smile on, do your face."' And whatever way she said that, it gave me a sort of warm, fuzzy feeling and filled me with adrenaline. She was right. I got up and put on a green jumper and for whatever reason, in that moment, I forgot Mum had died. I got in the shower, did my hair, and had a pep in my step for the first time in days. Then, within minutes, the house was falling around me again and I was talking about my dead mother. I sometimes left myself and had these lucid moments during that time. I kept pinching myself. None of it felt real. It was the most surreal time of my life.

We later went through Mum's belongings and it felt like such an invasion of her privacy. Her bank statements were among the things we went through, and to know my mum's account balance is something I'm so uncomfortable with. We found so many rosary beads, prayer books and mementoes from when I was baby – cards and telegrams congratulating my parents on the arrival of their son, the gift bag that contained my first blanket. For me, to find all of that, especially since I wasn't with her when she died, I wasn't able to touch her warm face … it was so nice to feel that I mattered so much to her. I was feeling her love at a time when I felt like I had completely neglected her. Mum and I always liaised on the phone – that was our main form of communication for 20 years, from the time I worked as an air steward in 1998 right through my life in London. In recent years, with social media, we were communicating even more via WhatsApp, Viber, Snapchat and Instagram, but we spoke on the phone at least three times a day. I've never opened the last message Mum ever sent me. It was through Snapchat, and I'd gone to bed without seeing it, and when I finally came across it, I'd already learned she was gone and couldn't bring myself to open it. Then I deleted Snapchat – I could never go on it again after Mum passed away. Later my sisters joked, 'What if that message said, "Help, something's wrong!"' My family always found great humour in such sadness. I can only assume that message would have been 'Goodnight'.

The morning my mother was found in her bed, my father had gone to work sometime after six o'clock and when he left, Mum was facing one way; then when Tara went to wake her, she was facing the other direction so she must have been alive when Dad left and turned over. I often wonder how Tara and her husband John, who was her fiancé at the time, coped with finding our mum like that. John tried to resuscitate my mother. Tara is the youngest and has since become a mother herself to my nephews, Harvey and Jesse. And I feel like our children – Tara's and mine – have completely missed out by not knowing Mum. All the other nieces and nephews – Chloe, Shannon, Sean, Leah, Sadhbh, Sophie and Rian – knew and loved their Nanna Rosie, while Harvey, Jesse and Blake, and if Arthur and I are blessed again with another child, those children will never experience that love from her and I'll always believe there's something missing from their lives as a result. Mum was like a second mother to Chloe, my eldest niece, who was born in 2001. Chloe grew up in my parents' home, so she was almost like a sister to us. Her mother, Tracey, had gone back to school in Sixth Year and Mum looked after Chloe for the first year of her life. After Mum died, Chloe and I were standing beside the coffin and I put my arms around her. Grief can be so self-indulgent – I'd only ever really seen Mum as my mother, I'd never thought of her as a wife, girlfriend or fiancée to my dad; as an aunt, a sister, friend, godmother or grandmother. When you step back and collectively look at someone's life, you realise there was more to this person than just who she was to you.

One thing my sisters said that resonated with me was that they thought maybe Mum died while I was in LA because she knew I was far away and was trying to save me from that trauma. To be honest, I don't know how I would have reacted if I was in the house that day: I don't think I'm brave. At the same time, I was angry that I was so far away when it happened, and I was on my own. Mum was teetotal for years, and weirdly, after she died I was suddenly disgusted by the taste of alcohol and couldn't drink. It made me feel ill. I abstained for the next two months, later to go completely the other way, drinking too much.

We found pictures of Mum when we were going through her things, and she was so pretty. When she was 21 and pregnant with me, she had long hair down to her waist. I'd never seen her like that before. Dad was really handsome, too. You can imagine how electric their relationship must have been. Mum was seven months pregnant with me when she married Dad. If they hadn't married, it could have ended very differently for all of us. In 1978 in Ireland, to be pregnant and not married, Mum could have been sent off somewhere and what would have happened to me? That will tell you the bravery my mother possessed. And this is where her pride comes from. When my sister Tracey heard people in the toilets at school calling her a whore and a slag for being pregnant at 16, my mum said to her, 'Don't let anyone speak to you like that. We're proud of you.' That's what my mother was like – traditional and yet so open-minded and loyal.

*****

I don't really remember the weeks and months that followed after Mum died, but that June, I turned 40 and my birthday party was going to be our first family outing following her death, the first picture we'd have taken of our family without her. I went to Las Vegas with my friends beforehand and I remember having moments of complete devastation, just thinking, *why am I here?* It was like car sickness. I was anxious and homesick, and I was masking my emotions with alcohol. It all culminated on my birthday. We were in House in Dublin and my friend Alan had given us the conservatory with a whole area in the back of the venue. It was the hottest day of the year. Arthur released 40 balloons for my mum, and it immediately sent me into a complete episode of catastrophic panic about my mortality – here I was at 40, my mum was 61 when she died, so I have 21 years left to live my life.

Pippa and Simon are usually the 'stiff upper lip' type, whereas my other friend, Leighann, is like me, very reactive in the moment – we're loud and not afraid to be passionate. And when the balloons were released, I looked over at Simon and Pippa and they were crying. I walked up to them and said, 'I expected more from you two.' I remember thinking, *how dare they do this to me?* Then I went over to the bar. There's a picture of me by that bar that no one has ever seen because my face is completely distorted. It's very scary. I look like I'm possessed. That photograph shows who I had become since the loss of my mother – I was a wreck, literally falling apart. When I look at that picture, it's so triggering. Whoever took it captured my soul.

That night, I took off my wedding rings and gave them to Simon saying, 'I can't do this anymore.' Simon grabbed me and took me to the bathroom and was like, 'Are you okay?' Whatever was happening in me, it was almost like I wanted to stop everything. And I just thought, *Arthur deserves better than what I am now.* I was in a state of panic – it was a family gathering, my mother wasn't there, I was 40 years old, my friends were crying, alcohol was flowing, I had to walk around and talk, I had to pretend …

There was a sit-down meal afterwards and Pippa was sitting beside me while Simon was just looking at me from across the table. I cried the whole way through that meal and Pippa grabbed my hands and said to me, 'You really need to get it together now.' It strangely sobered me. Within minutes, I felt I had come through it slightly.

I have flashbacks of Brian Ormond with his arm around Arthur, reassuring him that everything would be okay. No one else at that dinner knew what was going on.

The next morning, I was awoken at six o'clock by fire alarms going off in the hotel where we were staying and Arthur wasn't beside me. I knew he must have been there that night, as he would never leave me – no matter what state I was in – until he knew I was safe. Then I realised I wasn't wearing my wedding rings and the panic flooded in and I thought, *what have I done?* We all had to evacuate our rooms and head outside and that's when I found Arthur. He wouldn't look at me or speak to me. Pippa and Brian were standing beside me and suggested we all go out for breakfast. Arthur was reluctant but our friends persisted, and we all went to Balfes. I was so dehydrated. I had a Diet Coke, sparkling water, lime cordial, tea and a juice in front of me. Our friends were trying to lighten the mood and Arthur just said, 'I understand what you're going through, but your behaviour is erratic and unacceptable. I deserve more, and you deserve more.' I just sat at the table and started crying. I missed my mum so much. She and I had planned my 40th birthday together and she wasn't there to share it with me. This milestone was as much about her as it was about me. Arthur forgave me in that moment, we hugged and drove back home, and I was reminded just how lucky I am to have the most loving, wonderful, supportive husband, and I haven't forgotten that since.

The next month, I went to London and was almost afraid to sit down with Simon because he's the friend that would hold me accountable – as any good friend should. He said to me, 'We need to talk. I'm really worried about you. You can't be handing me your wedding rings and telling me you want "out". What do you want out of – your marriage, your life? What's going on?' He was concerned that I was drinking too much and my behaviour on nights out wasn't like me. He asked if I was okay and I said, 'No, I'm not okay.' To have my behaviour checked like that was a game-changer. It saved me from ruining my life. God knows what would have happened, what situation I would have gotten myself into had Simon and other people not spoken up. I had the best people around me at that time, and still do.

*****

My mother had a unique relationship with each of us. I suppose me being the only boy, gay and then on television – all of that made me very unique within the family. Mum and I weren't just mother and son, we were genuinely friends. I've never had an argument with any of my sisters, and that's because of our mother. Mum navigated all seven of us – each with different tastes and personalities – with grace and ease. She was a therapist, a chef, a nurse, an entertainer, and a best friend. She was all of that in one.

And Mum *loved* Arthur. She'd always tell me to appreciate him and wanted us to be together. Whenever I'd bring Arthur to the house, she'd make fresh scones or soda bread especially for him, saying, 'These are just for Arthur, nobody else is allowed to touch them!' When Arthur was moving to LA or travelling, she would say to me, 'This is wrong. You should be together, no matter where you are.' My mum always championed Arthur. After our break-up in 2006, she wanted Arthur to visit us at Christmas while he was in Ireland – dating a different guy. So, when we got back together in 2011, she was very happy.

Mum's perspective on money was very different from mine. She couldn't understand why I would go to Marks & Spencer to buy her a €100 coat when she could find a similar one somewhere else for €20. It's because she never had money to spare. When I was working with Ryanair, I bought her a jar of Crème de la Mer moisturising cream in Duty Free for Christmas. Mum would never buy herself expensive beauty products. Much later, I went up to her room to leave a bottle of perfume for her and noticed the Crème de la Mer was running low, so I said to her, 'You used the cream!' No, she had given it to my younger sisters … who put it on their dolls!

Years later, Arthur gave me a Louis Vuitton trolley for my birthday. I love big bold monograms because I'm thinking that if I've invested in a piece, the designer's name should be all over it. The bag must have cost over €3k, and I brought it home and Mum was like, 'You've more money than sense. That's ridiculous.' My nephew Rian, who was only three at the time, dragged it along the floor and scratched it. Mum just said, 'That's what you get for showing off. Why didn't you get a case down the road for €50? What do you expect?' That was her whole attitude. This was a woman who had to budget all her life, to feed and look after her family. She was a very proud woman. She never could indulge or splurge.

Our last Mother's Day with Mum, we brought her to London. We went to the Charlotte Street Hotel, where I stayed after *Big Brother* – it was my secret location and I wanted Mum to experience it. We were having afternoon tea, and I ordered another pot of tea for me, Mum, Aoife and Tara, and I think the extra pot of tea was £20. Mum went bananas. She just couldn't get used to that. My mum was born in the 1950s, and back then, I can imagine there were probably seven kids all in one room. While she was so modern and open-minded, she was still a little old-fashioned and couldn't just let go and enjoy a moment like that.

I had a great relationship with my mum and the tragedy of that day in February 2018 will never ever leave me. It's still so raw, five years on. Sometimes it feels like it was a month ago. And other times I'll wake up and think, what did my mum look like? On my phone, I had a picture of her on my home screen and one day, it suddenly disappeared and I couldn't figure out what I did to make it go away. I panicked. To be able to look at that picture anytime just warmed my heart and when I couldn't see her face, I felt so horrible … she was alive in that picture, and I was afraid it was gone forever.

When you go through a catastrophic loss like that, your perspective on life changes. Back in my twenties, I was quite entitled, almost taking my work and life for granted. Lately, I find myself just being so grateful. There is not a day that goes by that I'm not thankful for everything in my life. I used to always lie about my age, and now I'm 45 and realise I'm so lucky to be alive. Why don't we embrace ageing? My mum died at 61 – that gives me only 16 more Christmases, 16 more birthdays, 16 more Valentine's Days with Arthur, 16 more Father's Days with my child. I hope I live longer than that, but losing my mother made me realise every day is a gift, and I need to cherish every moment. I also used to be obsessed with my weight. Now, I can't remember the last time I stepped on the scales. In the grand scheme of things, why would I care whether my trousers are a size 32 or 34? I'm always either ten pounds underweight or ten pounds overweight, and I work in an industry where how I look is important, but since Mum died, I've never valued life more. If I discover a wrinkle on my forehead, so what? When I go to work, whether it's live television or live radio, and I make a minor slip-up or turn to the wrong camera – before I would have beaten myself up for such an error. Now, I just think, *we're not saving lives doing what we do.* We're in hair and make-up, wearing nice clothes and telling you what to watch on the telly or interviewing someone who's doing a new show. People who are saving lives, who are doing heart transplants, or paramedics – that's where it counts, and you can't afford to make a mistake.

Since my mother died, I've learned a lot about my dad, Gerry. I never noticed his sense of humour before – he can be quite funny. He's a great conversationalist and would tell us stories about the time he met Mum and what their relationship was like back in the day. I feel like my dad didn't really have a voice until Mum passed away. He was always working while we were growing up, and we went to Mum for everything. To see him step up in the way that he has is incredible.

I suppose I never felt for my father before because I was just grieving for myself. Dad called Michelle and me into the sitting room where Mum was in the coffin. He closed the door, and we had a private conversation. That was the first time I'd ever seen my father cry, standing over his wife's coffin. It must have been so hard for him to lose Mum. He wouldn't let us replace the bed in their room. All her perfumes, her hairbrush and skincare products are still on the dresser where she left them. Her clothes are still hanging in the wardrobe. Grief is so singular, and you're so caught up in your own feelings, you don't think about how someone else is dealing with their loss. And now my dad has a tough job because he has seven kids, and a growing number of grandkids, and he's learning birthdays and organising things at Christmas, and Mum would have done all of that. He's definitely changed and has had to be more present because the matriarch is gone.

Dad was only 60 when Mum passed away so he's trying to rebuild his own life now, and when someone begins to move forward that can be a tricky thing for other people in the family to deal with. He's still working and becoming more social, and it can be hard to accept that life eventually begins to move on after you lose someone when all you want is for that person to be alive. It's heart-breaking, and that's part of grief. You want the best for the person who's left without their partner, but you also want that person to be alive. It's just so sad. We wanted so much for our mum, but it's life and you have to fight to keep going.

*****

From the death of my mother arrived the podcast *Death Becomes Him*, which was something I really fought against doing at first. It was Easter of 2018, Arthur and I were back in LA, and Donal Skehan said to me, 'There's such vulnerability when you talk about your mother. The way you speak about her so eloquently, and the detail …' I'd not really spoken about Mum publicly because I was embarrassed. I felt so awkward on social media – I think I put one story on Instagram saying, 'Thank you for your support.' And Donal suggested I consider doing a podcast. I wasn't sure and didn't think anyone would listen to a podcast about grief. He said, 'Honestly, you could really help people.' I said, 'I'm grieving. If people hear how sad I am, they'll think I'm mad or depressed. I won't work again.' I thought my career would be over. People weren't talking about mental health in 2018 the way they do now.

It took some time for me to finally come around to feeling comfortable with doing the podcast, but I decided to give it a try and in December 2019, with the help of Cassie Delaney of Tall Tales, I recorded seven episodes, talking with Arthur, Pippa, Nadia, Nicky Byrne, Lottie Ryan, Des Bishop and my sisters. We planned to release those first episodes in March 2020, and then the pandemic happened and I wondered whether we still should, but in the end, we went ahead, and the podcast went to number one. I couldn't believe a podcast about death coming out in the first couple of weeks of lockdown would strike such a chord. Little did we know at that time what the world was going through. People were dying, and their loved ones weren't allowed to touch them or grieve properly. And, my God, I was not schooled in what I had with my mother's funeral – the church was full, the crowd spilled outside. We had the hugs, the handshakes – something I had resisted and resented at that time – and suddenly, no one had that. And I thought, *what is wrong with me?* I suddenly realised how fortunate we all were that we got to honour my mother's life and console one another. And how all of that did actually help me through it. If I didn't have any of that – the stories and the people telling me how amazing my mother was – what would I have been like?

Looking back, I probably should have seen someone to help me deal with my grief, but *Death Becomes Him* became a form of therapy for me. The day before I started recording the first episode, I wrote one line in my journal: 'Will I ever be the same again?' And that became the theme of all four seasons – it's that journey of exploring the question, will I ever be the same again? The answer is of course 'no', but at the time I wrote that line in my journal, I didn't know what the answer was.

Before doing the podcast, I hadn't really understood the power of a conversation. Mum fully believed that you can sit down with someone, no matter what you're going through – whether they betrayed you, you don't like them, you've got differences – and have a cup of tea and you can sort out anything. And conversations like the ones we had on *Death Becomes Him* don't age. If you listen to an episode in 20 years' time, it'll still be just two people talking about something so important. I wasn't planning on doing a second season but when I found myself going into season two, I sat down with John McAreavey and we talked about the murder of his wife Michaela on their honeymoon. I thought to myself, *I'm not a journalist, I work in entertainment, how do I know what to say about a case like this? How can I talk to someone about the murder of his wife when I've just lost my mum? What's the commonality?* Then John and I had a beautiful conversation and I found myself thinking, I *am* actually capable of sitting down with people, and the commonality is grief and loss, whether it's through murder, sudden death, accident, suicide: all of the people I spoke with, throughout all four seasons, were dealing with massive grief and I have a huge amount of respect for each of them. I feel connected to those people forever.

A woman contacted me after listening to the podcast. She told me how her mother was asking her to come over to try on an outfit for a wedding and she was putting it off. After listening to a few episodes, she got in the car in a panic and went straight to her mum's house. She felt so appreciative to still have her mother around to spend time with, and I thought that was so powerful. Just listening to the podcast made that woman realise how lucky she was to have that moment with her mum. Time is so precious. My life feels like it's going by so fast and it's so important to stop and take it all in, to cherish those moments.

I think the podcast resonated with people because death affects all of us at some point in our lives and it's something we need to talk about. I never would have thought an idea born out of my own selfish grief – to find out whether I'll ever be okay again – would help millions of people. It's one of the proudest things I've ever done in my career, and I know Mum would have been so proud, too. It was all because of her. I once had my nieces and nephews on the podcast and asked them where they thought Nanny is and they said, 'On a cloud, drinking tea and having biscuits.'

Doing the podcast, I learned a lot about strength, determination and fighting. You have to fight, and you have to make peace with what's happened. I fought every day since 2018, for my relationship with Arthur and to keep my head above the cesspit that is grief. And grief and I are in a really good place at the moment because it's not taking over my life now. I don't feel possessed by it. I had to make friends with grief. When you're friends with someone, they're not affecting you negatively. It's still accessible to me. It made me very hard and very angry at times, and I've never fully recovered from the loss of my mum, but now my grief doesn't bleed into other aspects of my life the way it did before.

But after four seasons, I needed to step away from the podcast and distance myself from death while Arthur and I were trying to have a family. I recorded the last episode in the summer of 2021, and it aired that November. I knew that when I was trying to bring life into the world, I couldn't be talking about death.

So much has happened in the last five years and yet, every birthday I've had since 2018, I've always thought something's missing, and that's my mum. Tara didn't have our mother beside her on her wedding day, and it was very emotional. She was the one who found our mother the morning she died. I don't know what that does to a person, and I don't know how I would have dealt with that. I think in a way, the fact that I wasn't there was a blessing in disguise, but I would never have wanted to have been so far away. Aoife was in London on her own when I phoned her with the news. It's so funny how it happened that neither of us was home at that time and Aoife went on to become our surrogate, putting us on this unique journey together.

The sad thing about loss is that life does go on, and you have to move with it or you get left behind. Mum would always emphasise how important life is, and one of the things to take away from *Death Becomes Him* is that you have to live your best life for the person who's gone; otherwise, their death meant nothing. You have to fight. And it is a fight because there were days since 2018 when I couldn't get out of bed, but now every day I get up and put my feet on the ground, I think, *aren't I so lucky to be alive?* Equally, don't be afraid to ask for help, to say 'I'm really struggling'. That's not a sign of weakness, it actually takes great strength, power and courage to do that. And never underestimate your family and friends – being surrounded by the right people is so important when you're coping with grief ... and throughout your one short and precious life.

7

BRIAN AND ARTHUR:

From LA to Ireland

From 2018 to 2020, the two of us did our best to get our lives together back on track. It was a challenge and there was no clear answer as to where we would both be happiest, but we just kept putting one foot in front of the other and the most important thing we had was our love for each other.

*****

BRIAN

When Arthur returned to LA in the summer of 2018, for the first time in my life, I really felt the need to get on a plane and go to my husband, to put his needs ahead of my own and be by his side. It took my mother passing away at 61 for me to realise life is too short, and that I needed to live mine differently. Mum would always say to me, 'I don't mind the fact that Arthur's in LA, I mind that you're not with him. You're a married couple, you should be together.' It was always my mother's belief that no matter where we were, we should be together, and I wanted to honour her wishes and cherish the life I had with him.

But while my heart was pulling me to be with Arthur, America was his dream, not mine, and I was still grappling with the longing to be near my family in Kildare. I knew London was no longer an option for us – Arthur felt he'd accomplished everything he wanted to there, and my apartment in Clapham was rented out to a tenant who would eventually go on to buy the place. I was so emotional moving out of that flat – I remember being on my own, packing everything up and thinking, Arthur and I were together here, we fought here, we were intimate here, we had all our moments in this place. I was broken-hearted. It was the first place I'd ever bought. Even during the times when I couldn't afford to pay the mortgage, those four walls were everything. They'd seen me through the highs and lows, and closing the door on that felt so sad. I remember going to the toilet on the plane back to America and just having a complete emotional break-down, thinking, *I've walked away from my home*. It was the fact that my mum had sat on the sofa there. And once you have a stranger living in your place, renting it, it's no longer your home. I was walking away from Abbeville Road, from those early years with Arthur, after 14 eventful years.

In the coming months, I travelled back and forth between LA and London, and Ireland too. I did 14 long-haul flights that first year. If I'm completely honest, deep down, I think I always had a plan to try and get Arthur and me back to Ireland after my mum died. I felt this pull to home that I hadn't felt before – I would never have thought back when I left Ireland in 1998 that I'd want to return one day for good, but I was a different person now, and Ireland was a different place.

In 2019, Arthur and I were invited to take part in *Ireland's Fittest Family: Celebrity Special*. At first, we turned it down – it would have involved a lot of travel back and forth. When I told my sister Aoife, she said to me, 'You know that was one of Mum's favourite shows, don't you?' I'm not sure why I didn't know that but as soon as she said it, I immediately got on to my agent and apologised, saying, 'I've changed my mind, I want to do the show.' We started recording and Adam Byrne, who's Nicky Byrne's brother and a producer on *Dancing with the Stars* in Ireland, was on the set. He'd heard I had turned down an offer to be a contestant on *Dancing with the Stars* and told me he thought I should reconsider, that I'd be great on that show. I later got a call from my agent asking if I would be interested. I'd been offered that role before but turned it down and once again, I told my agent I didn't think it was for me. Once again, Aoife chimed in and reminded me that *Dancing with the Stars* was another one of Mum's favourites. Then Mairead Ronan, who was the host of *Ireland's Fittest Family* at the time, said it could be a great opportunity to raise my profile amongst Irish audiences and open more doors for me here – I had really struggled to work in Ireland prior to that. I got offered the odd job but it wasn't enough to sustain a career. I was more successful in the UK. So I thought it over. I realised the more opportunities I'd get in Ireland, the more I'd have to physically be there. And this decision wasn't just about my career – I'd be doing this for my mother. I called my agent back and asked if it was too late for me to say yes. I was so lucky – they were still happy to take me. Larry Bass, the CEO of ShinAwiL – the production company behind the show – said he'd make it work if I was really sure. One thing I really wanted was to have a male dance partner, but the show had already been fully cast – they'd just managed to squeeze me in at the final hour. I was told if I wanted to take part in a same-sex dance, I could do it during Switch-Up Week. So it was decided: I was going to do the show.

I started preparing for *Dancing with the Stars*, and it was so hard. As I've mentioned earlier, I have a real issue with being touched and people coming into my personal space. I don't like it. And when you're dancing, you can't help but be close to your partner. You're physically grabbed, your legs are slapped ... I remember saying to my dance partner, Laura Nolan, 'I can't do this, it just doesn't work for me.' She put me at ease and said she'd help me get more comfortable with the moves as we practised. It was great to know I had Laura's support and understanding.

And yet I had numerous meltdowns doing that show. Mum loved *Dancing with the Stars* and wanted me to do it, and I never did while she was alive, and now I found myself going through this awkward experience every week publicly. I was feeling so vulnerable, and I didn't want to be vulnerable in public – I thought if I did that, I wouldn't get work. People would think I was falling apart. Who was going to take me seriously then?

I rang Arthur saying, 'You've got to pull me out of this.' I wrote numerous emails to Larry that I never sent saying, 'I can't do this anymore. I'm so sorry.' And Arthur just said to me, 'Man up! You're so lucky you have this.' And I thought, *he's right*. I picked myself back up and got on with the job and the next thing I decided was that I needed to get to week six because the following week was Switch-Up Week, and I was determined to use that opportunity to do a dance with a male partner. I approached all the male pros and said, 'I need to know now if you would have an issue dancing with me if I make it to Switch-Up Week.' Once I knew I had their support, I just had it in my mind that I needed to get through each week so that it would happen, and I finally got there.

When I look back on my early TV career, I'm reminded how incredible it was that I won *Big Brother* as a gay Irish man, and that I won it twice. Then being on *SMTV Live* at 23, it was culturally phenomenal that I was able to do that as a gay man. I didn't understand that at the time. Cut to 2020 and I was on *Dancing with the Stars* in Ireland, doing a same-sex dance with Kai Widdrington. That had never been done before and by then, at the age of 41, I understood the power of that, that this was a monumental moment. We went on *The Late Late Show* the night before, and I knew I had to get this right. I knew the language I used had to be accurate. This was such an opportunity.

Kai and I were dancing on a bridge in Dublin at eight o'clock on a Tuesday morning in February. We were doing a photocall to promote that week's episode ahead of it airing. It was freezing. We were wearing these Dolce & Gabbana sequinned jackets with nothing underneath, jeans and Gucci trainers. Kai and I had never held each other before. I was so nervous. Crowds were on their way to work, and we were getting beeps and waves. It was lovely. I told Kai I was really cold and he put his arms around me, gave me a hug and rubbed my back up and down. He said, 'I know you're nervous and I know how important this is to you. I have you, you're good.' Five minutes later, we were flying through the air. We were in hold. It was so important for me to get it right. It was frosty, people were beeping, hollering and waving, and I just thought, *how amazing that I live in a country as progressive as Ireland has become.*

The night of the live Switch-Up Week episode, we were doing the quick step and we danced separately first, and when we got in hold together, face to face, frame to frame to run around that ballroom, I just felt it from the audience. I received a message from a woman whose 16-year-old son came out to her that weekend after watching us. She said she knew now that he was going to be safe, that he would be accepted. That cemented my belief that doing that dance with Kai was so important.

In a way, I'm glad I didn't know in my twenties the pressure I was under being a gay man in the public eye. I didn't really have a voice when I joined the *Big Brother* house, so how was I supposed to express myself? Even with interviews, I was always very mindful not to bring up the gay thing. It's so weird. The opportunities I was given when I was young were rare, but then I was getting those opportunities again later in life, which was good in a way, as I took it more seriously. And as much as I had people advising me, I was making my own decisions. I was calling the shots. I was using the words that I felt comfortable with. Because when you're 23 and living in a city where you don't know anyone, you're on a massive television show, working with celebrities, interviewing people like Beyoncé and Jennifer Lopez – that's already a lot to process at such a young age.

When Will Young won *Pop Idol* in 2002, I knew exactly what he was going through. Like me, he was a young gay man who'd just stepped off this huge reality TV show. In his own book, Will reflected so eloquently about me, saying he didn't feel I was ever given the respect or credit I deserved, doing what I was doing as a young, openly gay man. And it was only when I read that, that I thought, *actually, he's right.*

Doing *Dancing with the Stars* was so bittersweet – I was missing Mum the whole time. My six sisters danced on stage with me for one of the episodes, which we dedicated to my mother. I finished the show in the middle of February and by then, there were all these rumblings about the Coronavirus going around. I had plans to head over to the States to join Arthur but couldn't fly because of the pandemic. Arthur's work, meanwhile, was also being affected by cancellations, and then he was advised to leave LA because he didn't have a green card, only a three-year visa.

So, we set in motion plans to get Arthur back to Ireland, and once we were together, staying in my childhood bedroom in Rathangan, I knew I had everything I could ever need. The only thing missing from our life together now was a family of our own, something we were both determined more than ever before to make happen.

*****

ARTHUR

I will never forget the snow that fell in March 2018, less than a week after Rosie's funeral. I was due to leave Ireland but got stuck there. We joked that it was Rosie – she didn't want Brian and me to be apart again. Eventually, the snow melted, and I went back to LA, but for the next two years, Brian's heart just wasn't in to moving to America anymore. He'd come over and have meetings but then go back to London for work. He was always being emotionally pulled back to Ireland, to his family.

Meanwhile, things were really opening up for me in LA. I was only there about six months when I got a phone call to audition to be an expert judge on the talent show *The World's Best*. Funnily enough, James Corden, who was in my car a few years earlier, was hosting. It aired in the US after the Super Bowl in 2019.

I knew there was something broken in Brian during this time. I wasn't going to force him to live in LA; I knew it would take some time before he was ready to follow me. But I missed my husband, I wanted to be with him. I wanted us to build a family together. America was my dream, but I could tell it wasn't what Brian wanted.

Brian had been grieving for two years and I felt like it was time to move forward with our lives. We had meetings set up in the US to look into adoption. I didn't want to go down the surrogacy route there as I knew there were so many children who needed a loving home, and surrogacy in the US was so expensive, into the hundreds of thousands. So we were gearing up to start our life together in LA.

We were both busy working – Brian was in Ireland doing *Dancing with the Stars* at the start of 2020 – and next thing, Covid hit. That changed everything. My work suddenly came to a halt. I didn't know what to do. We were still on a visa. Our friend Donal Skehan contacted the Irish embassy for advice, and they told him, 'If you're Irish and you're on a visa, if you don't have a green card, leave now while you can because we don't know what's going to happen.' That triggered something in me. I suddenly felt this panicked feeling and the need to be with Brian. Donal made the decision to move back to Ireland with his family. I was torn. My head was saying, *I don't want to leave LA.* I was just getting started and loved it there. But my heart was telling me I needed to be with my husband. On 15 March 2020, everything shut down and I called Brian to tell him I was moving back to Ireland with Donal. At the time, I figured it was only temporary. We didn't know what would happen. I just knew I needed to be with Brian during all of this. Our visa was for three years so I thought, *we'll stay in Ireland until everything dies down and once things reopen, we'll go back to LA.*

The day after I called Brian, I was frantically trying to pack up our entire apartment and talking to my mum, telling her the news that I was moving to Ireland for a while. She asked, 'Do you love Brian?' I'm like, 'What do you mean? He's my husband, of course I love him.' She said, 'I was just asking because I know how much you love America and how much you wanted to be there. I just want to be sure you're making the right decision.' My mum is honest and knew what I was giving up. I boxed up all our belongings in three days. It was really scary. I was running around wearing a mask, documenting everything on social media and making arrangements to travel back to Ireland with Donal, his wife Sofie and their two boys. We put everything in a container, which took about four months to get there. Flights were being cancelled but we just made the best of the situation and kept our hopes up that we'd get to Ireland before everything stopped. I just wanted to get to Brian. It was the first time I can remember ever feeling that need to be physically with my husband. It was such a weird moment. We finally arrived at the start of

April ready to self-isolate and then Brian and I moved into his parents' house, into his childhood bedroom with our massive bed that I had brought back from America, which took up the whole room. It was honestly the best thing that ever happened to us. It was the first time in 20 years we had spent that long together. Ireland was either going to make us or break us. We just got on with life like everybody else.

We were living with Brian's dad, Gerry, his sister Tara and her fiancé John and son Harvey, who was one year old at the time. We were creating memories together. I figured it would be a few months and we'd eventually go back to LA, but the pandemic lingered on.

By the following January, everything was shut down again and Brian and I moved into a new house in Straffan – not far from the Dowling family home in Rathangan. By then we'd realised we weren't going back to America and decided to start building a new life for ourselves here. We had grown accustomed to being together all the time in the same place, near our nieces and nephews, Gerry and the Dowling sisters, and to head back to the US now just didn't feel right. Ireland had become our home and we were determined to put down roots.

At the same time, I was left wondering what I was going to do – I didn't have a career in Ireland. No one really knew me here. I always joked, though, that I'd rather be living somewhere I was happy and working in a café than be living somewhere I was unhappy doing what I loved. And once I was living here, I fell in love with Ireland and its people. During the pandemic, I created TikTok videos of us dancing and just being silly and people followed our story on social media.

Of course, me being me, I couldn't help but think, *what next?* I was frustrated and needed to channel my energy into a new project I could get stuck into. That's when I came up with the idea for my collection of unisex socks: The AG Official. I created the logo, and working with a design company, designed the look of the socks. Brian couldn't believe at first that I was making it happen. It took two years to launch because of the pandemic but it kept me busy at a time when life felt like it was standing still.

People have always underestimated me, but I am a doer. I've had to fight for everything I've achieved in life and I'm always pushing myself. At times, perhaps I've been naive and pushed too much, but that's okay – we all learn from our mistakes and any mistake I've made has led me to something else. I really do believe that everything happens for a reason.

To this day, I don't regret the move to Ireland one bit. We were meant to be here, and I know that now. Our lives took a new turn once we were living here together and we've never been happier. In June 2021, I was in Kerry with friends and got a call from Eugenia Cooney, who is a producer on *Dancing with the Stars* Ireland, asking if I would be interested in auditioning to be a judge on the show, signalling the start of yet another new chapter in my life.

I agreed to do the audition but didn't think in a million years I would get the job. Several weeks went by and I got another call in August asking if I would come in to do a screen test. I was shocked – and I don't normally get shocked.

I went in for the screen test in September and suddenly spotted a whole bunch of familiar faces in the room – people I've worked with who are friends. I was auditioning for probably one of the biggest jobs of my life, but I just wanted to be myself and go for it. The screen test was all a blur. I thought, *I'm not going to get this.*

And at the same time, Brian and I were making serious plans to start our family, dealing with all the heavy stuff like clinics and doctors, so my head was all over the place. Everything was happening all at once. It didn't feel real. We were in deep and wanted so badly to have this baby. I really didn't think I'd get the job. There are dreams you can dream but you know they're not reachable. Brian is a realist, and I'm an optimist, but there have been moments in my life when I was a realist. This was one of them. It was a primetime TV show in a country where they speak English; I'm a foreigner and my English isn't particularly strong – I thought, *there's no way I will get this.* Then I got a call from Eugenia at the end of October. I was in the kitchen, and I remember she dragged it out with this long dramatic pause … 'You got the job.' My heart was pounding. I was starting yet another stage of my life. I couldn't comprehend what was happening to me. I had a flashback to a time when I was talking to Bruno Tonioli in 2006 where he said, 'Anything could happen.'

Brian was worried for a while thinking I'd moved to Ireland for him and there was nothing for me here, so when he heard the news I got the job, he was so relieved and happy I'd found my own niche and could shine on my own. And that was a good feeling for both of us.

I'm not going to lie, I was very nervous … not just about sitting in that chair, but how people were going to take it. I discovered I was replacing one of the judges, and it's always nerve-racking when you're replacing someone – you're always going to be compared to that person, no matter what.

I don't normally get nervous. As a dancer and a chore-ographer, I've never been nervous because I know what I'm doing. When I sat in that chair for the first show on 9 January 2022, Jennifer Zamparelli and Nicky Byrne started talking to me and I decided I was just going to go for it. They knew who I was, I didn't hide anything, so I just enjoyed the ride. I wasn't there to step into anybody's shoes. And thankfully, the reception I got was extraordinary. I couldn't believe how supportive everybody was. And that gave me the confidence I always knew I had. I realised, *I can do this*. I never doubted myself, really. I thought, *I can present a show*. With a little practice, I can do anything. That's my mentality.

Some people in Ireland knew me from social media but *Dancing with the Stars* opened so many more doors to the wider public and a new demographic knowing who I was. I'd meet fans of the show who'd ask to take their picture with me – and not just Brian. That felt nice.

A week before I debuted on *Dancing with the Stars*, we found out we were expecting our first child. I could not stop crying. I was like, *can this get any better?* I was buzzing every week from then on sitting there in that chair because I secretly knew we were having a baby.

The pregnancy came about in the most surprising of ways after we were left wondering what our options were now that we were living in Ireland – adoption here as a same-sex couple wasn't looking likely – but life is all about surprises and I've always believed in allowing life to take me where I'm meant to be. That said, if Ireland didn't feel right for me, I wouldn't be here. To me, happiness is number one. After my dad died, my mum said to me and my sister, 'Be happy!' That's always stuck in my head. And now, in my new home with my new life and loving family, I have finally found my true happiness.

8

BRIAN, ARTHUR AND AOIFE:

Straffan, County Kildare, Ireland

BRIAN

I t was January 2021, a couple of days after New Year's, my sister Aoife had been staying with us, and she and I headed out for a brisk walk to shake off the cobwebs of the festive week. The air was cold and fresh, and it felt good to be out of the house. I was thinking about our plans for the future, now that Arthur and I were living here permanently, and Aoife and I started talking. I told her I didn't know what we were going to do – how were Arthur and I going to be able to have a family here? Our options felt so limited. Where would we start? Aoife turned to me with a serious look on her face, she took my hand and said, 'I've been thinking long and hard about this and I've done some research. You two aren't going to be able to do this on your own.'

She explained that she wasn't sure she would ever want children of her own, but with all our sisters having gone through pregnancy, she wanted to know what that felt like, and more than anything, she wanted to help Arthur and me to have the family we so desperately wanted. I said to Aoife, 'Are you mad? You're single, you're young, why would you do that?' Her voice was breaking, and she replied, 'Brian, you're not taking me seriously … you two have done so much for me and I really want to do this for you. Please respect that this is what I want.'

When I asked Aoife how this would even work, she had all her answers ready … firstly, she wouldn't be using one of her own eggs but that of a donor. Her only request was that she could deliver the baby via Caesarean section. That's all she asked. She knew far more about surrogacy than I did. I was so touched and so impressed by how strong and determined Aoife was. Could this really be my baby sister?

The two of us returned home from our walk and said to Arthur, 'We're having a baby.' Arthur just looked at us confused and said, 'What are you on about?' I explained that Aoife wanted to be our surrogate and Arthur was stunned – tears filled his eyes and a huge smile appeared on his gorgeous face. He was so happy. We had a big group hug and then sat down for a cup of tea to discuss our next move.

I always wanted a family, but in my mind, I didn't see it as a realistic possibility, so I didn't allow myself to consider that as my future. I was an uncle and a godfather. When it came to being a parent, I figured it wasn't going to happen for me – I'd love for it to happen, and always thought, *if a baby arrived at our door, wouldn't it be amazing*? I also wasn't sure I'd ever be a good dad. I always believed myself to be spoiled, independent and self-indulgent. I'm also my own worst critic.

I'm lucky that Arthur was so adamant about us having a family because I was fixated on all the other stuff like getting the new job and a bigger house – at the end of the day, I was just giving myself excuses. It was fear. I was afraid that if I invested so much time into this and we didn't have a baby in the end, I'd be broken-hearted. I was trying to save myself from being hurt. That longing of wanting a baby and then getting close to it or focusing on it emotionally and financially and then it not happening was something I didn't think I'd be able for. I protected myself by saying, 'We're self-employed – how's this going to work?'

It wasn't until after I lost Mum that I realised I really wanted a baby. I thought, *what are we doing with our lives?* A week after the funeral, it was snowing outside, and I told my sisters that Arthur and I were going to have a family – that I definitely wanted to make this happen. Little did I know then that three years later one of those sisters would be offering to bring that baby into the world for us.

At first, the whole idea ruffled some feathers in my family. My sister Michelle came around to the house when we first told everyone our plan, obviously with great intentions, saying that the family had had a conversation and they didn't think it was a good idea because they were worried about Aoife and her mental health. And I lost it. I stood up, the table rattled, and I just unleashed this tirade. My whole point was, when Tracey got pregnant at 16, who gave her permission? I stood by Michelle,

Valerie, Tracey, Paula, Tara – all of my sisters – when each of them got pregnant. When did I come around and tell any of them that this wasn't going to work? It was the first time I'd ever had a cross word with my sister. I was crying, Michelle was upset, and we left it at that. It was all fine in the end. Their concern wasn't about me wanting to become a father, they supported that; they were worried about our sister.

I wasn't sure how it would all work legally, so I went online and started googling and spotted a solicitor, Annette Hickey, in the news who specialised in surrogacy law. I contacted her for advice, she came back to me straight away, and Arthur and I then spoke to her over FaceTime. We were very vulnerable opening up to this complete stranger about our desire to have a family and she couldn't have been more supportive. She guided us through the ins and outs of the current legislation in Ireland, what we could and could not do, all the potential pitfalls and what we needed to do to protect ourselves on this journey. It was in equal parts overwhelming and reassuring. The next step was to find a clinic that would work with us, which proved challenging.

The whole process of providing our sperm samples was something I was deeply uncomfortable with. I said to Arthur, 'I'm not going into a room at the clinic to have someone see us and know what I'm doing and say, "Is that Brian Dowling in there?"' There was no way we were doing that, so we chose to carry out that step at home. I thought perhaps Arthur and I should do it together in an effort to make it somewhat romantic … believe me, it's not romantic! You're given these little cups that you have to put your semen into. I jokingly suggested we try to 'arrive' together at the same time. We both then started laughing and it brought me back to the juvenility of our early relationship … and here we were now, in our bedroom, masturbating into two cups because we wanted to have a child.

All of this was going on at a time during the pandemic when you couldn't go a certain distance beyond your house and we had to get the sample to the clinic within 30 minutes because it had to be a certain temperature. I said to Arthur, 'If a member of An Garda Síochána stops you, you whip out those two cups of semen in the bag and you tell them, "My husband and I are trying to have a baby – we have to go to the clinic!'" It was all systems go, and then we waited patiently for the results.

Then we were dealing with the hormones and trying to help Aoife's womb reach the necessary measurement. It got to a point where Arthur had to insert the medication into Aoife vaginally to increase the chances of it working. She was lying on the sofa, cushion under her bum, we were watching a movie, I paused it to fetch tea and chocolate, Aoife had her legs wide open and Arthur had a plastic glove on. That's what we did – there was no glamour in it.

*****

ARTHUR

Ever since I was 16 years old, after the death of my father, I have wanted children, to provide them with the stability and experiences I didn't have as a child, as well as the affection my father wasn't always able to show me. Hearing the news that Aoife wanted to be our surrogate, I was shocked and elated. I said to them, 'Is this a joke?'

I couldn't believe the gift she was prepared to give us. Brian explained that Aoife was adamant she wanted to do this and we all just started crying.

We had so many questions, the first being, where do we start? Then Brian discovered Annette Hickey and that was the beginning of our long journey. She was amazing. She talked us through all the logistics and details, the pros and cons of this and that, how we couldn't do certain things here and where we couldn't go and where we could. I didn't care what we had to do, I was on this journey and I knew we had our surrogate, someone who was going to carry our baby. That was the main thing, but there was so much information to absorb.

The biggest roadblock was that we couldn't carry out the embryo transfer in Ireland because of the lack of legislation around surrogacy. No clinic here could help us. It was very disheartening. Then we learned of a clinic abroad that someone else had used for surrogacy and we contacted them and met a lovely gentleman over Zoom who said he'd help us. We needed to find an egg donor, but the good thing, he said, was the fact we had a surrogate, as that's usually the biggest challenge people faced. Before we could get started, we all had to do lots of tests – me, Brian and Aoife – to see if our sperm was viable, and if Aoife was healthy enough to carry a baby.

The clinic had a strict policy that an embryo transfer could only be carried out once the surrogate's womb reached a measurement of 9mm – this was to ensure its success. We struggled for months to get Aoife's womb to measure that size. All the hormones and all the medication she was taking were not working. We measured six times unsuccessfully. And every time we'd be so excited going to the clinic, only to then find out it wasn't there yet. That was really hard, and Aoife was starting to panic. She was like, 'I'm so sorry. I'm the problem.' And Brian and I were like, 'Don't you ever apologise for anything – you have done nothing wrong; this is not your fault, you are giving us this enormous gift.'

Meanwhile, we also had to find our egg donor. That was another task, and it was weird going through all the donor options, trying to decide. You don't actually know what these women look like, you just have a number and a very detailed file about who they are, right down to their physical features as well as information about their parents and grandparents, but you don't see any photographs. We told the man at the clinic we ideally wanted someone who was tall so that narrowed things down a bit. We finally narrowed it down to three potential donors and then we had a Zoom call with the guy at the clinic and he asked if we'd made up our minds yet. And Brian – being Brian – said to him, 'If you had to take one of these women out to a bar on a date, which one would you take?' The man blushed, took off his glasses and said, 'In the twenty years I've been in this business, no one has ever asked me that before.' He laughed and gave us his answer and the two of us said, 'Then that's the one.' So we have him to thank for that as well. Our donor was studying medicine, very intelligent and well-educated. That's about all we know about her. The clinic suggested we administer the hormone medication vaginally to improve the chances of it working. Aoife was working in a hotel at the time and bless her, she would go into the disabled toilets on her break and lie on the floor for 15 minutes while trying to take the medication. But it wasn't working. We realised she needed help with this, so I stepped up – let's face it, Brian wasn't going to do this. I have a strong mind and I've seen it all before. Aoife came to stay with us, I put the gloves on, took out the two tablets, Aoife's legs were in the air. *Boom!*

Still we waited for her womb to grow to the size it needed to be. We were nearly at the stage of giving up, because we were worried this was all getting to be too much for Aoife. The clinic then suggested we try going by the natural cycle – to stop the medication and allow Aoife's uterine lining to thicken in accordance with her natural ovulation cycle. This was our last attempt, and I swear, someone was watching out for us because we measured between 7.5mm and 8mm with the natural cycle. We called the clinic, and they said it was a good sign and that by the time we'd get to the clinic at the rate we were going, we should be measuring 9mm – enough for the transfer. We booked the trip to the clinic. Brian had to work so he had to stay behind, and Aoife and I got on a plane on 17 December 2021. My heart was beating so fast, and I was filming everything, trying to document this whole journey. We were so excited.

Two weeks prior to that, we had got a call from the clinic saying that unfortunately, one of our embryos, which had split into twins, had a chromosomal abnormality, and the clinic – as a duty of care to all involved – only uses the healthiest, most viable embryos, so we only had one embryo left to work with, who was our beautiful baby girl. At the time, hearing that news, Brian broke down, he was so upset. We had just one embryo for the transfer, but we just tried to stay positive.

I arrived with Aoife to the clinic on the 17th and she was 9.5mm. They told us to go and relax in our hotel and come back on the 19th for the transfer. When we returned two days later, they showed us our embryo, which was six days old, and it was so energetic – like a Tasmanian devil. They told us it was time to go for the transfer and I will never forget, I filmed Aoife as she was walking through this long corridor. I went to the lobby to wait, and finally Aoife came out. Now it was a waiting game. We went back to our hotel, and Aoife lay down with her legs in the air for four hours. This was our only shot – it had to work.

Aoife had a craving for mango, and I went all over town trying to track one down. I would do anything for her. Throughout everything, she never complained once. Funnily enough, we turned on the television in our hotel room and the Junior Eurovision finals were on, and who won the contest but Armenia … I took that as a sign.

We travelled back to Ireland the next day. It was such a scary journey – we couldn't help but feel like somebody was going to stop us. Throughout everything, though, Annette Hickey was our golden ticket. She looked after us and guided us. We then had to wait an excruciating two weeks before we could do a pregnancy test. It was so stressful and exciting at the same time.

When I first told my mother the news that Brian and I were going to have a baby, and that it would be carried by Aoife, she was so surprised and immediately worried about Aoife, saying, 'Are you sure Aoife is 100 per cent certain she wants to do this?' Once I assured her everything was fine, she was totally behind us. In fact, my mum was the first person to suspect we were pregnant. She came to visit us at Christmas, and we were having a glass of champagne. Aoife was the one who opened the bottle and as soon as she smelled it, she felt nauseous. My mum said, 'You're pregnant, I know you are.' We had a blood test scheduled, but the night before, on 30 December, Brian said he wanted to do a pregnancy test. I said, 'Don't jinx it.' I waited downstairs, my heart pounding, while Aoife and Brian were upstairs doing the test.

The blood test later confirmed what we hoped and now the next stage of worry would begin because Aoife was pregnant. We'd now need to start antenatal care in a maternity hospital, so we'd need to find the right doctor for us. Pippa recommended the doctor who delivered her children, but he was set to retire by the time our due date arrived. And then we were put in touch with the secretary for Declan Keane at the National Maternity Hospital. She explained that it doesn't matter who we are or what our circumstances are, it's all about the baby. We met with Declan Keane, and he addressed Aoife throughout – because she was the person carrying our baby, she was the patient. It was very awkward at first, but we got used to it and Declan is one of the best humans on the planet. He took such good care of us all and explained everything. He was so gentle and reassured us every step of the way.

*****

BRIAN

Because I couldn't attend the embryo transfer, I wanted to have a role in all of this, so I said to Aoife, 'You're going to pee in a cup and I'm going to do the pregnancy test myself.' I sat on my own and put the stick in and the second line came up straight away within a second. And I was the only person that knew we were pregnant, that I was going to be a dad, for about two minutes. I then came down the stairs where Arthur and Aoife were waiting, screaming, 'We're fucking pregnant!' It took us a year to get here, and anyone that has gone through any sort of fertility issue or that is struggling knows the toll that can take. Two men trying to have a baby is no mean feat and we were now a huge step closer.

I went in for the first scan when Aoife was just over six weeks pregnant. Arthur was on a shoot so he couldn't join us. They said to me that even though Aoife's test came back positive, there was still no guarantee we were going to see a baby or hear a heartbeat. And at every stage, you're never guaranteed anything. We had the first ultrasound and I presumed it was going to be the gel on the tummy like you'd see on TV. It wasn't – it was a vaginal scan, and I was unaware of this, and they put this massive camera inside Aoife.

Keeping the pregnancy quiet until we were ready to share the news was difficult. We'd been married seven years, and once I revealed in an interview our intentions for having a family it then became this thing we were constantly asked. That February, we were going on *The Late Late Show* to talk about Arthur's role on *Dancing with the Stars* and I said to the researcher, 'We're not going to want to deny anything, so please don't ask us if we're pregnant.'

I was so worried for the whole nine months. God knows what it must have felt like for Aoife, every time the baby kicked and moved. She was just incredible. So strong, so focused, an absolute trooper – through the hormones, the ovulation kits, peeing in a cup … right through the difficulties of pregnancy: her changing body, stretch marks, the carpal tunnel, her bad back. Thankfully, she didn't experience morning sickness – that was one small blessing. But she knew there was a lot of pressure on her.

There was a lot of talk and gossip from people about Aoife that was just horrendous. My sister Tara's hen party was in

January 2022, just after Aoife became pregnant, and we were well aware, given the occasion, that people might pick up on the fact that Aoife wasn't drinking and begin to suspect something. There was lots of speculation about Aoife, that no one had seen or heard from her and later on they saw pictures of her wearing a loose-fitting dress at around 12 weeks and thought she might be pregnant. Rumours were flying around but we just didn't pay them any heed.

When we finally announced we were pregnant on social media at the start of May, we posted the video Arthur took at the moment I screamed the news to him and Aoife, who was there with us in the room, but we chose to edit her out of that video as we weren't quite ready to reveal the identity of our surrogate, and I can be heard in the video using the words '*We* are pregnant'. Oh, the hate I got for that. That's when it all started. We got messages calling us rapists, paedophiles, nonces; saying things like, 'With enough money and a cruel heart, you can buy a baby,' 'You're the same as the Magdalene Laundries but you're the ones that are buying the babies,' 'How can two gay men bring up a child?' These were comments people placed underneath the sonogram of our daughter.

I wasn't expecting our announcement to be on the cover of the newspaper, if I'm honest. I think we underestimated the amount of interest there would be, good and bad. Then the suggestions started spreading that we were taking advantage of someone in a poor country. And I realised, they don't know that it's my sister who's carrying our baby.

At work, Aoife was hiding the pregnancy. We managed to get a lot further along than I thought we would before announcing that she was our surrogate. Then Aoife was starting to show, and people found out. Some told her she mustn't be happy and asked, did she not want to keep the baby? I told Aoife, 'Tell them the dad is married and that should shut them up.' We officially announced that Aoife was our surrogate in a gorgeous video that Arthur put online, with Celine Dion playing, just a few days after our initial pregnancy announcement. Aoife was wearing a beautiful dress and looked amazing. That eased the hate a bit.

The rest of the pregnancy was kind of a blur for me. And then we started shooting the documentary *Brian and Arthur's Very Modern Family* for RTÉ, covering our surrogacy journey right up to the birth. I asked Arthur,

'Are we absolutely stupid for doing this?' I worried we'd get more backlash, but it received a wonderful reaction in the end from viewers. People still message me about that documentary saying they were so moved by it. I think the one thing people see when they watch it is just love.

Aoife showed me who she is through all of this – that she is the most amazing person I know. I have so much respect for anyone that does what Aoife did for us, anyone who is a surrogate for anyone, in any country all over the world. If it weren't for my amazing little sister, Arthur and I wouldn't have our family.

9

BRIAN AND BLAKE

Our beloved daughter, Blake Maria Rose Dowling Gourounlian, finally arrived on 1 September 2022. It was a day the two of us, and our extraordinary surrogate Aoife, will never forget. As film crews were documenting the birth, the two of us were experiencing a thousand emotions – worry, fear, joy, sadness, elation, awe and an unbelievable sense of love.

The day my daughter was born is a day filled with so much joy but also such sadness and worry. Despite how far we had come to get here and all the support and guidance from the team at the hospital, not to mention Annette Hickey, I couldn't help but feel like someone was going to walk into the room and take Blake away from us at any moment. I didn't even want the nurses to take her for a bath, as I was terrified that she wouldn't come back. At the same time, my sister was in another room and I was so worried about her. I was feeling I needed to be with my newborn and Aoife at the same time and I couldn't be in two places at once. I really felt for my sister not having our mother beside her through all of this and I was so emotional.

But even on the day of delivery, Aoife never wavered. The moment Blake was born, I was standing beside Aoife, who said to me, 'Go to your daughter. I've got this.' I was really torn. I was 44 years old and just wanted my mother. There were two of us in this – a brother and a sister – and we both wanted our mother, so I had to be Aoife's mother, father, brother and best friend.

I did skin-on-skin with Blake first – it felt wonderful and yet so strange to look at this miracle child of ours in the flesh. And then we had to do a DNA test to prove which one of us was Blake's biological father so that person could be put down on the birth certificate. That felt so degrading – we already knew who Blake's biological father was and to be honest, it's so irrelevant. So much pressure is placed on that minute detail, and it actually doesn't matter.

Arthur was so in touch with how I was feeling. I was holding Blake and I said to him, 'I need to go and check on Aoife.' She's my family and I had to make sure she was okay. If something went wrong, if anything happened to her, I couldn't forgive myself. I was actually upset for her when I learned she had stretch marks but she didn't care herself. And she recovered so well from the birth. Straight away, she was so coherent and asked for her phone. And a few hours later, Aoife held her niece for the first time. It was a really special moment and one we felt needed to happen in Aoife's own time.

When we left the hospital with Blake, we had to carry an umbrella to block anyone from taking our picture. That sounds very dramatic, I know, but we were just so protective of our little baby girl. It was the strangest thing walking out of that hospital as a family of three. People were beeping at us and waving. We were so happy, but we were also so sad. Arthur and I cried the whole way home. We were so emotional because we had left Aoife, who was placed in this room where mothers would go if they were bereaved, if they'd lost their baby. She was still bleeding, and I remember saying to Arthur, 'What have we done?'

I felt so low. I wanted to take Aoife from that room and bring her home with us. Leaving her in that hospital was the hardest thing we had to do. I honestly wondered in that moment if we had ruined my sister's life; it really was heart-wrenching. I struggled so much with it, and yet we had our child. Halfway home, we stopped the car and just wept. We couldn't breathe. Blake was asleep in the back of the car and we were so afraid. I felt so vulnerable and missed my mum. When we finally arrived home, we Face-Timed Aoife and were still crying and she just laughed. She assured us that she was okay and we needn't worry.

Then Arthur and I lifted Blake out of her car seat and reclined on the sofa and Blake slept on my chest and I said to Arthur, 'If we could just stay here forever, just the three of us like this, I would.' It was just that sense of being home. Then I thought, *how are we going to do this?* This was uncharted territory.

But I needn't have fretted. Blake was such a good baby from day one. She only ever had one night-time feed. We'd feed her at 11 p.m. then put her down and she'd go four hours until three o'clock. She'd be up and back down within 30 minutes and wouldn't wake again until after eight in the morning. This was one instance where we felt grateful to be self-employed, as we could feed her and get right back into bed. Arthur would always get up, though, as he was constantly on the hustle, working for our family, but I could remain in bed with Blake until her next feed at 11.30 a.m. It was bliss.

There's nothing more attractive than seeing your partner be the parent you want and need them to be. For the first six to eight weeks after Blake was born, I didn't sleep for fear that something was going to happen to her. I'd be constantly making sure she was breathing. Arthur is so positive – being with him is like being with Mickey Mouse. During those early weeks, even though Blake was so easy, I was adjusting to being a parent and it was at those times when I was so tired that Arthur was so amazing. He'd just step in, coping with the same amount of sleep as I was. He still does that now whenever I need to be working. I think when your partner steps up in life, you truly see why you married them. Sometimes we take people for granted, whether it's our partner, family or friends and we need to remind ourselves now and again how fortunate we are to have them in our lives.

The first time I took Blake out and about by myself, the two of us went shopping and I was so proud and yet so nervous I'd do something wrong, that she'd cry and I wouldn't know how to soothe her. What would I do if it rained or a bee appeared out of nowhere? I'm so clumsy, what if I tripped? What if I couldn't work the buggy? I think everyone who saw me that day knew I was anxious and they waved at me from a distance to put me at ease.

I was an exceptionally nervous first-time parent, so I needed Arthur to allow me time to adjust to some of the daily tasks I was afraid to mess up. The first time I tried to bathe Blake in the sink she was slipping out of my hands and I was panicking. I have an irrational fear of water so could never get in the bath with her. I didn't change any of her dirty nappies in the beginning because I was too scared, wondering if I'd be able to manage – even though I'd looked after my nieces and nephews, I'd never dealt with a poo before. So Arthur would change all of those until about two or three weeks in, when I finally decided I needed to be able to do this and stepped up. Now, I've mastered it – when she goes, it's up her back and it's no problem for me, I'm there. I was just anxious about everything at the start but Arthur balances all of that out. We've always complemented each other in our personalities, even as parents. I'm good cop and he's bad cop. When we need to be a bit stricter with Blake now, Arthur's able to step up, whereas I'm just a bit silly with her. She doesn't take me seriously. The two of us have mastered the art of tag-teaming by now. When Arthur was gone every weekend for 12 weeks working on *Dancing with the Stars*, I was holding the fort with Blake. And when I started working on 98FM doing daily radio slots, Arthur swooped in to take the reins.

During all of this, Arthur and I have developed the utmost respect for single parents. I don't know how they do it because you can lose yourself in parenting. We're very lucky that a lot of our friends and family have children so we had their support, understanding and guidance the whole way.

To be honest, I wish I cherished those first few months of Blake's life more at the time. My one regret, if we never have another child, is that I missed relishing her being so young because I was so afraid something bad was going to happen. I couldn't believe we were so lucky to have her.

I really do think she's a miracle in every sense of the word.

I've learned so much since Blake came into our lives. Firstly, I've discovered that I can do way more with my time. Time before was something I filled with stuff that was in no way important to my life. I'd stay up until one o'clock in the morning watching television and was filling my life with stuff that didn't really benefit me. I've found that since Blake's arrival, I'm managing my time better, doing far more with it than before. Blake has made me a lot softer, too. I'm definitely way more emotional. She's also made me a constant worrier. I think that comes from a combination of losing my mum and having a baby within the space of five years – two really big life changes that have left me fretting about everything.

When Blake was eight months old, Arthur and I took her on our first holiday abroad as a family to France to visit Arthur's mum and sister. After three days, I had to return home for work ahead of the two of them, and it was only then, standing in the airport alone, that I realised I was probably suffering trauma from my mum's passing. I was in a different country when I received the news of her death. Before she died, I never feared anything bad would happen when I lived in a different country to her, but since Mum passed away, whenever I go to an airport, I'm so anxious. It only triggered when I left Arthur and Blake that Sunday in the South of France. We awoke that morning to the smell of freshly baked croissants. Blake had slept well and we were all in good spirits. But I couldn't eat. I knew in my stomach I was going to an airport and saying goodbye to my daughter and husband and was filled with anxiety: *What if this is the last time I see them? What if something bad happens to me on the flight? What if something bad happens to one of them?* I never questioned my mortality before – I never questioned anyone's mortality before, but when you go through a traumatic, unexpected loss, it makes you question everything. I'm not living in fear – I think I'm just living in a reality where my happiness can be taken away from me at any point. I have no control over it. And it was something I'd never realised before.

The same things I felt losing Mum, I've felt having a child. It's the same real-life worries – but life happens. I don't want Blake to ever get sick or go to hospital. I don't want her to ever be bullied. But that's life. I don't want her to ever fall but she'll have to fall because she'll need to learn how to get back up. It's all these little life lessons. I don't want her to have her heart broken, but she needs to have her heart broken to know what love is really like. She needs to be treated badly to know how she needs to be treated correctly.

*****

My sister Tara's wedding was two weeks after Blake was born and we all went to that wedding – me, Arthur and Aoife. We had such a great time. I didn't get to bed until half past four in the morning. Aoife was still recovering from the C-section, and it was so lovely for her to be able to share those conversations with my other sisters about pregnancy because she was the only one who hadn't experienced it before then.

We all got ready together and my dad was so proud that day. We brought someone with us to look after Blake and that was the first time we didn't have her with us when we slept. It felt really strange. We got criticised for having someone at the wedding to help us, but what do you do?

Our newborn needed to be cared for and it was my baby sister's wedding – I wanted to be there for Tara. And we were fortunate enough to be in a situation where we could get someone to help us for a couple of days and still spend time with our daughter.

As much as it was my sister's wedding, I was very aware that no one had ever seen Blake before that day or knew what she looked like. Blake had not been on our social media. We just wanted to keep our daughter to ourselves for a while and live in our own little private bubble. So at Tara's wedding, it was the first time people saw me and Arthur as parents as well as Aoife after being pregnant. There was a lot of pressure on her to keep it together because she was bound to be emotional – she'd just had a baby. And Aoife was just an icon – she handled it with such class. She was almost regal while holding Blake in her arms.

My family is really good at being united. We close in and are at our strongest when we know people are gunning for us or have an opinion. And I'm sure there were some people at that wedding who were judging us. And my sisters were like, 'We don't care. We love our niece. We love Aoife. We love you. We're so happy.'

I've done a few collaborations with baby-care brands in the first year of Blake's life. I was so excited to be a dad and represent same-sex parents. Blake wasn't in any of that stuff in the beginning because she was so young, but later when I did one job where I worked with Blake, I was told by someone that I was prostituting my child for fame and money. Let me tell you, anything I've done since 1 September 2022 is for my child. Everything we do is for her, everything we have is for her. We are sharing our experience of parenthood because we are so happy. If I get opportunities to work and support our child, I'm going to say yes. And if we're asked to have Blake included, as her parent, I'm going to say yes until we get to a point where I think it doesn't feel right for her.

When we went on *The Late Late Show* with Blake, we were criticised by some for having our baby up so late. And when Blake cried on the set and I went to pick her up and she immediately stopped crying that just showed anyone who doubted us just how loved and happy she is. And to have Aoife sitting beside us on that sofa, looking so classy and handling herself so strongly talking to Ryan Tubridy, and to hold that whole interview together, I was so proud of her. To have that moment with our daughter and Aoife was incredible and one day we'll show that to Blake.

Blake is a 'fuck you' to anyone who trolled Arthur and me or doubted our ability to be her dads because she is the happiest, healthiest, most loved baby there could ever be. Whenever anyone sees our daughter, she is smiling, laughing and thriving, and it's proof to everyone that all a child needs is love, regardless of the parents' gender or sexuality or if that child has just one parent or guardian. If no one knew that Blake was born to two dads, and that one of their biological sisters was their surrogate, and you lined her up with three other children, how could you pick her out as the one who had two fathers?

The stuff that was said to us – we were called paedophiles, womb rapists, nonces, child traffickers. Arthur didn't know what a nonce was and when he googled it, he was horrified. To call someone a paedophile because they want to be a parent, just because they're gay, is horrifying. It amazes me that people still associate homosexuality with paedophilia. I don't understand it. It shocks and sickens me. I don't know what is so horrendous about

Arthur and me wanting a child. We often hear stories in the news about heterosexual people hurting and abusing children, yet in some people's twisted minds, when you're gay you're automatically guilty of being a nonce.

The trolling was so dark sometimes that I began to fear being out in public with Blake, that we'd be attacked on the street while walking our baby in the pram. You can tell me to brush it aside, that it's to be expected when we're living in the public eye and sharing our lives on social media, that we bring it on ourselves, but do we really, to that level? It's still hurtful. It stings. Just because I share my life with people online, why should I expect to get hate? I don't understand that mentality – because you put it out there, you should expect negativity. That's *that* person's problem. People who are hurt go on to hurt other people. Anyone who's ever attacked us, they're sad themselves.

I used to think it was a sign of weakness to block someone or remove messages. It's not a sign of weakness – it's choosing to focus on the positives and I'm too busy to reply to toxic people. Now I block because I'm not going to allow these people to see how fabulous my life is. You are not going to see my gorgeous daughter. But

I do believe that a lot of people have a duty of care, that if I do an interview with a publication, and they put it up on Instagram and it gets a comment from someone calling my husband or me a nonce, that publication has a duty of care to delete that message. I don't need to see that. It's not because I'm weak. My daughter, when she gets older, doesn't need to see that. And other people don't need to see that. Haters shouldn't be given that platform, nor should the people who chime in with their own comments to that message. As soon as someone says something negative, people who support us go in for the kill. These are strangers we've never met who have our backs and we're grateful.

There were also a lot of people who had so much concern for Aoife, that I was taking advantage of her. They were painting our egg donor and Aoife as victims. They're not victims. We don't know our donor, but to my knowledge, this was something she wanted to do. She wasn't forced into it. And Aoife is definitely not a victim. She is strong and knows what she wants. And now she spends so much time with Blake, minding her and taking her for walks. For us to have Aoife in Blake's life is priceless. Blake has two dads, but she also has an aunt who was her surrogate so when Blake has the sort of questions any child might ask their mother like, what was it like when I was in your tummy? We can say, *let's ask Auntie Aoife.* We're delighted Blake has access to that.

Arthur and I had to fight to have our family. I'm constantly left wondering, *when do I have to stop fighting for the things other people take for granted every day?* Throughout my whole life, I've had to fight more. I had to fight to come to terms with my sexuality. I had to listen to people's opinions about me. I had to fight to be taken seriously in my career, to get married as a gay man, to have a child. And here we are again, having to fight to get both our names on Blake's birth certificate. It's constant.

The whole process of trying to have our child has been one of the most challenging aspects of my life. And in a country where one of us is not recognised is heartbreaking. What defines a parent? What's different about two people who get up every four hours to feed their child, who take turns sleeping, who change nappies throughout the day, who both love their child unconditionally? Oh, because one has DNA that gives them priority over the other. And if anything was to happen between Arthur and me, how one of us could take our child away from the other is devastating. If our relationship was to end, one of us would be left stranded. And it's not just about the two of us – doesn't Blake deserve to have both her parents' names on her birth cert? It's her legal document – shouldn't it represent her family, her identity? Arthur and I are with her every day of her life. We *love* her. Why should one of us be on that document and not the other? And why is my sister's name on it when she's Blake's aunt? Aoife doesn't want to be Blake's legal anything. The fact that when Blake was born Aoife had to sign a document giving us permission to have a say in Blake's medical care was absurd to us. We were assigned a social worker in the hospital, who we had to talk through everything with. They were all doing their best in a very unique situation, but at the time it felt so degrading. And Aoife cried, saying, 'Stop referring to this baby as my baby. She's not my baby; she's my niece. I'm not her mother.' Especially during her recovery, it must have been so difficult for Aoife to deal with all of that. She was paranoid that everyone would think she had postnatal depression. It was only after we all went on *The Late Late Show* that Aoife started to get trolled on social media with people saying things like, 'How can she give away her baby?' It was never her baby. Why can't people simply respect Aoife's decision? Why do people feel the need to paint Aoife – or our egg donor – as a victim? Why do people always choose the negative option? When men give a sample of semen in a clinic for money on their lunch hour, they're almost high-fived. A woman does the exact same thing with her eggs and she's a victim. It's so hypocritical. People say we should all be treated the same, but we're not treated the same. The fact that someone's response to Aoife saying she's not sure she ever wants children but she'd like to experience pregnancy was, 'Oh my God, how could she say that?' But why *can't* she say that?

When we started filming the documentary, I wasn't sure if Aoife wanted to be involved, so until I was sure she was comfortable, I protected Aoife from all of that. Then Aoife said she wanted to do it and just before we started shooting, I said to the production team that they could have a word with her. Once the cameras started taping, I think the production team realised that this girl is sassy and so independent. She's so strong and the documentary showed that. There's relief in the fact that it's since aired and people can see that Arthur and I are living a very normal life.

Someone once asked me why I wanted to be a dad. I thought, *am I supposed to be pitching my life to you?* Arthur has been asked the same question and it makes us so uncomfortable. Why does anyone want to have a kid? Would a heterosexual man or woman be asked that question? The desire to have a family isn't reserved for straight people. Growing up as a gay kid, I really believed marriage and a family was the preserve of those who are heterosexual but I've since discovered that just isn't the case – it just doesn't come easily.

I'm delighted to now see the surrogacy legislation in Ireland finally getting the attention it needs, that things are changing. I live in a country that put obstacles in place for me to have a family. We had to travel to another European country just to get medication for my sister because a doctor wouldn't prescribe it in Ireland for fear of being struck off because of the lack of legislation. Isn't that ridiculous in this day and age? If we were a hetero-sexual couple, we could have fertility treatment. It just amazes me. Ireland is progressive but there's still so much that needs to be done for everyone to feel included.

Arthur and I were very aware during our surrogacy journey that so many other people have fought for the changes that are now afoot. They opened the door for us, even though it was still a struggle. We're thankful for the work of people like our solicitor Annette Hickey and all those who are online, marching and fighting daily. They deserve our respect.

*****

Blake has been a game-changer for all of us. She's helped me mature and made me unafraid to push myself. She's brought me a new lease of life and given me a hunger for the career I've chosen. Blake has given me the courage to be able to say yes to things I was once afraid to do, and to be honest and vulnerable and live my truth. She reminds me of my mum.

Blake is like my little best friend. I can't wait to grow old with her and see what she accomplishes. I can't wait for her to walk, to go to school. And honestly, she makes me want to be a parent again, to have another baby and not be so worried this time. I was so afraid to take everything in with Blake because I thought it'd be taken away from me. I sat in that hospital the night she was born gripping her crib and wouldn't let go. I was paranoid that someone would take her. My sister was in a room on her own, my husband was asleep on the floor and I thought, *if someone comes in wearing a uniform, what are we going to do?* Even leaving the hospital, I kept worrying. I don't think we're going to rest fully until *both* our names are on Blake's birth certificate.

Every day, I am mesmerised by who my daughter is becoming – her individuality, her little personality. She's a bit of a tomboy, not a girlie girl in any way. Once upon a time, I would have thought I'd want my daughter to be girlie, but now I don't care – I just want Blake to be her wonderful, expressive self. Blake really is just love. She's such a ray of sunshine. She doesn't complain and just loves life. And I know it's physically impossible, but she really is the best of Arthur and me in one little person because she mirrors the both of us in everything she does.

I'm 45 now and, having a daughter that's so young, I'm constantly thinking about the future. I want to be around for her forever, to see her get married if that's what she wants to do. I'd love to be a grandfather one day if she decides to become a mother. Blake has made me want to live, to be as old as I can be. She's made me want to fight harder. She's made me want to be more successful and happier. I feel I need to be the best version of myself for her. She's given me another shot at life and brought so much love into my world, which was already great to begin with. I never thought I could be this blessed.

Blake has restored some of the love I felt was missing in my life after losing my mother – I really feel like Mum has sent Blake to us. I never thought I'd be excited again after Mum passed, but Blake has brought so much light back into my life. She has opened my eyes to all of life's wonderful possibilities. With Blake, I just see so much hope and potential. I do fear for her, having two dads. I feel selfish for wanting her so much and putting her in that situation. But if anyone ever judged her or treated her differently because of her parents, I'm confident she'll be equipped to deal with that because I think she's going to be such a well-rounded individual. She's shown me love, support, fear, anger and vulnerability … every possible emotion. Blake has also shown me just how strong Aoife is – my sister, someone I probably didn't give enough credit to.

I'm thankful for my daughter every day, and grateful for my life. I would never have thought I'd be living back in Ireland with my husband, raising our child together. It's so far removed from what I thought I wanted. As a parent, I do want to instil in Blake the kinds of values and traditions that I had. I know that in this day and age, it'll be a challenge, but I'm just going to do my best to raise her with kindness, patience and love.

*****

I haven't shared this before now, but I've thought long and hard about it and have come to the conclusion that it's so important that we talk about things like this. During our journey to start a family, I found out that I'm infertile, and it was devastating for me to hear. It's something I have been quietly dealing with throughout the whole pregnancy and ever since our daughter was born.

I received a phone call from the clinic, and they said they thought the sample was 'off'. They thought initially it was because of something else. At first, they thought I had cystic fibrosis, which panicked Arthur and me, but my age didn't add up to cystic fibrosis because I've never had any other health issues. I then had to go for genetic testing and that took precedence over everything else at that time. My infertility was so bad that my doctor asked me how much chemo I had as a child, and I had to tell him I'd never had chemotherapy. They were so perplexed as to why there was just … *nothing*. I waited weeks for the genetic testing and that thankfully came back all clear – there was nothing wrong with me. I'm just completely infertile. Arthur and I have joked since then that there will only ever be one of me, but when you're told you're infertile, and you're trying to have a family, it's very hard. People have since questioned Blake's DNA or shared their opinions about who she looks like, and that's often triggered me a little bit.

The funny thing was, the same person called me and Arthur within 50 minutes of each other, so he and I were actually crying on the couch because we thought there was something more serious at play – that there might be something wrong with my health. And they told Arthur he had super sperm! I started to laugh, but there were also tears. I suppose that made everything easier, though. Our surrogate was my sister. Even though we were using a donor egg, if I had been Blake's biological father, because Aoife's name was on the birth certificate as Blake's legal mother, that would have caused all sorts of confusion with the registrar – if they didn't know our situation, they would have thought it was a case of incest. The guards might have been called. So things have a way of working out.

There were procedures I could have gone through, but the chances of me having something viable were very slim. And how lucky were we that I was married to Super Sperm? We didn't need to worry about getting donor sperm as well. Aside from my sisters and a few very close friends, we've never told anyone who Blake's biological father was … until now.

If I'm being 100 per cent honest, during the pregnancy, I did have those doubts in the back of my mind, wondering will I genuinely love this child the way Arthur does. I was so emotional towards the end of the pregnancy. I remember the day she was born, I held her and I didn't feel anything straight away. I was in awe of this child but I was waiting to feel this whoosh of emotion. Then I went out to fetch a McDonald's for Aoife. It was really an excuse for me to leave the hospital for a short break because it was all very overwhelming. I found myself unable to cry so I started playing really sad songs to try and make myself feel something. I did the same thing in 2018 when Mum passed away and I couldn't cry. I was so numb. And I was like, *I love her – of course, I love her.* It wasn't really until I brought Blake home that it finally struck me – I remember just holding her in my arms and going, 'Oh my God, you're my *child*. You are my daughter.'

I'd get paranoid when people would say, 'She's the image of Arthur's mother.' There were people who sent me messages like, 'Stop denying your daughter's biology.' And I'm like, *why are you messaging me this? What is wrong with you?* No one's denying anything. I don't think Blake needs to wear a T-shirt saying, 'Brian is my dad' or 'Arthur is my dad'. It doesn't mean anything. It's an odd one to navigate when you have strangers telling you your child doesn't look like you, she looks like her other father. Also, no one knows what our egg donor looks like.

It was always only going to be one of us that was Blake's biological father, anyway. My situation just cemented which one of us it would be straight away. Infertility was something Arthur and I never considered. It's the ignorance of youth – the assumption that, being a man, I'd always be able to father a child.

The fact that I'm infertile is something I'm okay with now. I've come to terms with it, but I won't lie – it was very hard for a while to accept. I'm actually embarrassed to tell people I'm infertile because I know how cruel and nasty people can be. And I don't want to put myself in a situation where people are laughing at my inability to have children. I don't want to give people sticks to beat me with and another reason to hate me because we've just taken on too much already, and that's the God's honest truth. I'm still a man.

People could always assume who Blake looks like, but until now, I didn't want to give people the whole truth. I thought, that's for Blake to know, and I don't want someone telling her about me being infertile and who her biological father is. I really struggled with the decision as to whether or not to tell this story, but I just hope in sharing my fertility experience, it might help someone else who might be going through something similar.

And now that it's out in the open and everyone knows, perhaps people might stop with the speculation, and we can all get on with being a family.

10

ARTHUR AND BLAKE

The day our daughter was born is one that is stamped on my memory forever. The nurse came to take Aoife to get her ready for the C-section. Brian and I were in the room, and I was feeling so sick in my stomach but trying to be brave. I didn't know what was going to happen. How could I? I'd never been in a room when a baby was being born before. Like every other new parent, I was feeling very nervous – and I'm not usually a nervous person. I don't panic. Everything I do, I'm just like, *it's fine!* But that day, I was nauseous. I remember walking into that room and seeing Aoife lying there and I just went into a haze of bewilderment and worry. I couldn't remember what happened after that until I watched the documentary later. I was crying so much.

I remember a few little things, but I was very frustrated. This was the moment I'd been waiting for my whole life.

And then when Declan Keane showed us our daughter, it was a very *Lion King* moment. Blake didn't make a noise, she literally came out silent and then suddenly she sneezed and had her first cry and we were so relieved. It was the best thing. I was squeezing Aoife's hand and I couldn't breathe and then everything was a blur. Now, after watching the documentary, I can remember we cleaned Blake and took her into the other room. Then Brian asked permission to hold her. I said, 'She's your child, of course you can hold her!' Brian was the first one to do skin-on-skin, and then it was my turn. I felt her warmth on my chest and it was the most magical feeling in the world. It was like the beginning of something stunning, something beautiful, something gorgeous in my life. I don't think there are any words that can adequately describe that feeling. Amazing, incredible ... that feeling you have holding your child that you have wanted for such a long time. And knowing how we got there is just beyond belief.

We were filming the documentary throughout all of this and when the camera crew left, Brian and I just stared at our daughter. We were also panicking because we thought somebody was going to walk in and say, 'I'm sorry, we have to take her away.' I remember a nurse came in to change her and we said, 'No, that's okay, we'll do it!' We didn't want Blake out of our sight. We were doing everything ourselves. I was sleeping on the floor and Brian was sleeping on the bed. We didn't want anybody to touch her because we were paranoid that somebody would take her. And throughout it all, I just kept smelling her. It was wonderful. That was an experience I will never forget.

*****

Since having Blake, my life has certainly changed, but for the better. I don't really remember what I was doing before she was born – I was very busy, I know that. My routine now is so different, and it's all dictated by her. And I love it. I want to be healthy so I can watch her grow up. There's so much ahead of her, so many experiences she'll have, and I want to be there for as much of that as possible. I'm still the same person, but my priorities are different. I still want to go out, but now I look forward to coming home to her.

I love looking after Blake. This is what I've been waiting for all my life. Being with Blake, looking at her face, is the best thing in the world. I don't remember much from when I was young so I want to create memories with my child that she will cherish forever. That's why I'm obsessed with taking videos and pictures – I want to document all of these amazing moments in our lives to look back on.

Blake is so clever. Now I understand what Irish people mean when they say, 'She's an old soul.' It feels like she's not a baby but a 79-year-old woman inside the body of a one-year-old. The way she is looking at you, the way she's smiling and teasing. She already has such a personality. She knows what is right and what is wrong and what she needs. I think she's going to be feisty. We both keep saying she's not going to be a girlie-girl. What I love about her is that she's got this energy that we needed. Both of us are so loud and full of life. I think she's a combination of me and Brian together. She's got a big personality – bigger than life.

And all of this has brought Brian and me closer than ever before. I think it started back when we got the news that we were having a baby. Then again, we've survived so much and we always came back to each other. But Blake has definitely brought us even closer together. I'm gobsmacked by everything Brian has taken on since our daughter was born – all the jobs he's doing … he's exhausted but he's doing it all for us, for our future. He takes a bus at seven in the morning every day to be on the radio but it's all for Blake. Everything we do is for her. She is our purpose in life now. Brian wasn't an emotional person before Blake came along. Now, every time he leaves her, he's crying. When his mum died, he was emotional, but it was different – he shut down and blocked his feelings out. Blake changed all that. He's an emotional wreck now. I'd never seen this beautiful side to him before. He's always been patient, but I think having Blake has brought out all those feelings he's been keeping locked up until now. He's become softer.

My mum is obsessed with Blake – and Blake just lights up whenever she enters the room. My mum hasn't been well in recent years – she's had cancer twice – and it's been hard being so far away from her, so we try and visit with her as much as we can, especially since Blake was born. Mum would never tell me if something was wrong because she doesn't want to worry me. She's been through so much in her life that I think she's so used to carrying all her burdens and not allowing her children to help her, but I wish she would let me support her the way she's always supported me. She's 75 this year and I feel like maybe she believes she's accomplished everything she set out to in life now that her children are happy in theirs. She's done everything for us but not for herself. So I worry for her, and we talk every day. She's a huge inspiration to me. And I see so much of my mother in Blake. They are so alike. I am grateful that the two of them have each other to know and love – these two amazing individuals that mean so much to me.

*****

The homophobia we experienced after we announced the pregnancy was soul-destroying. You're in this positive bubble of joy and then all this hate comes at you from strangers who don't fully understand your situation. People said we were disgusting and said things like, 'You're not pregnant, your surrogate mother's pregnant.' Then once we announced later that it was Aoife who was our surrogate, we started getting really positive messages of support saying, 'This is the most beautiful thing ever.' But I will say, I never experienced trolling and homophobia like that before. It was eye-opening, to say the least.

Some of the things that were said made me feel sick to my stomach, but I don't allow it to get to me – I just rise above it and move forward. But Brian will let those things get to his heart. He's more emotional than I am. He would get upset and feel the need to respond, but there's no point – you're just opening yourself up for something else that you don't need to read later. Thank God I'm strong-minded. If I wasn't, I'd have a very hard time reading all of that and not letting it get to me. I just think to myself, those people don't dominate my life, they don't pay my rent, they don't buy the food on my table, they don't dress me, so I don't really care what they say or think. It's their opinion: it's horrible, it's disgusting, but it doesn't matter. One message that did get to me, though, which I didn't understand at first as I wasn't familiar with the term, was when we were called nonces. I don't engage with people like that. Yes, it angered me but I'm over it –

because who is this person sending this message? You go to their profile and there's nothing there. Like, show your face. They're just nobodies hiding behind a screen. They're only keyboard warriors because they will never say the things they put online to your face. So I don't give them the attention they're craving. They're not worth my time. I have a child to raise and a job to do and a husband to make happy; I don't have time for trolls.

There were other people who asked us questions like, 'Why would you want to have kids?' I don't understand how anyone could ask that question. Why shouldn't I want to have a family, just like my own parents did?

You can block bad comments on Instagram if you want to, but I don't want to do that because it's kind of hypocritical as I choose to put myself out there. We live our lives on social media, I post about my daughter every day, so it would be inconsistent of me to avoid the backlash that comes with that altogether. But if I was really down or it affected my mental health, I would probably stop the bad comments from reaching my eyes. Because every time somebody attacks you, that kills you, little by little.

My daughter is growing up in a social media world, where you need to know how to use an iPad and a computer; if you don't, you're lost. So I want her to learn, but I want her to be very confident and be like me, to rise above it and not worry about anything that's said. It's just words. I know words can be very harsh, but these people are not your friends. These people are not in your life. Just move forward. And it's not just social media anyway – people go to work or school and get bullied all the time. It's across real life. So I will educate Blake to be strong – that whatever she reads, she needs to rise above it. I think Brian is learning that and becoming stronger than ever. He'll see something online and get angry and I'll just go, 'Have a cup of tea. Let's move on. You can't take it seriously.' That's what I tell everybody I know. There's always going to be someone out there who's going to criticise you. You can't make everybody love you. It doesn't matter who you are or what you do. Everybody's got different tastes and opinions. Whoever loves me, I'm privileged to have in my life and grateful for those people. Whoever doesn't love me, doesn't matter. Don't follow me if you don't like what I have to say or how I'm living my life. Why are you taking your time to follow and criticise me? If I don't like someone, which never happens – I love everybody – but if I didn't, why would I take my time to say something negative to them? I love my life – I'm not going to waste it sending negative comments to some stranger.

And that's what I'm learning with Blake. I'm very protective but I want Blake to learn about the real world, the same world I grew up in with everything I've been through. Her childhood will be very different from mine, of course, but that's not to say she won't have her own struggles. I don't want to cocoon her too much. I want her to learn from her mistakes. Brian and I have both made our own fair share of mistakes and come out the other side. I want her to know there are bad people in this world but there are good people too, and some people fall somewhere in the middle. Resilience is so important to have, and I want that for Blake.

My mum always said, 'It doesn't matter where you go, what you do or who you meet, always say hello, thank you and goodbye.' Those words always stuck with me and as her parent, it's something I want to instil in Blake. I want her to be kind and polite because that's how I was raised.

I also want her to find herself. I want her to experience things. We all grow up wanting to do things our parents don't want us to do. Now that I'm a parent, I understand the frustration parents have wanting to just keep their children safe. I will of course encourage her to be careful but what she ultimately decides to do is her choice. She needs to build resilience. Of course, I'll be scared and worried about her, but I'll have to just hope that she's intelligent enough to make the right decisions, and I will constantly guide her in the right direction. I think Brian will be the softer one. I'll be the bad cop, but in a good way. I'll be the bad guy but also her best friend. If she wants to do something, I'll encourage and support her because my mum did that for me. She never stopped me. My policy is: you don't ask, you don't get; you don't try, you will never know. I want to have adventures with Blake. I cannot wait for her to walk and for us to go places together. I want to create so many memories for her doing things I never got to do when I was young.

To the people who've doubted our ability to be parents to Blake, all I would say is, 'Have you seen my daughter?' She is the happiest, most content human. Raising her is the thing I am most proud of in my whole life. Every parent is new to the role when they have their first baby, and we're no different – we don't know what we're doing. We're literally going with the flow. It doesn't matter how many people send us links or books – I've never read a parenting book, I don't watch YouTube videos on how to feed my baby. I'm winging it. And I won't tell someone else how to raise their child. Those bullies, those horrible people who trolled us – they should watch the videos and pictures we post of Blake because then they will see for themselves that this is one content little girl. She's well, she is fed and she is always smiling. So we must be doing something right.

*****

Everybody's surrogacy journey is unique. This is our story and, hopefully, by sharing it, it'll help others to know what is possible but equally that it's really difficult. It was by no means easy. We're not advocates for surrogacy – you won't find us marching or campaigning, we just wanted to have a family. If our story helped to shine a light on the reality of surrogacy, the reality of the many different families who need to turn to it to realise their dreams; if it's helped people to understand it and helped legislators to realise how urgently we need the legislation brought up to date to help so many families stuck in limbo; then that makes us happy and proud to have played some part in all of that. But there are many people who have been working so hard to bring surrogacy legislation to Ireland, and we have those people to thank for helping us to realise our dream.

Again, I firmly believe that everything happens for a reason. Every time something happened along this journey, it was the right thing at the right moment. Losing the embryo that was twins was meant to be because we mightn't otherwise have Blake now. I always try to find the positive in everything.

We are so privileged, so lucky and my sister-in-law has given us the best gift ever. I will never be able to repay her. I first met Aoife in 2003. She was a baby back then. Who would have thought that little munchkin would end up carrying my child nearly 20 years later? Our bond is incredible. She's just the best and has grown so much. Brian and I were both very worried about Aoife throughout everything. Equally, I knew how strong she was. Once Aoife was pregnant, she became a different woman overnight. She matured so fast. It's like something switched in her head. I think carrying Blake has changed her perspective on her own life now. And what she's done for us is absolutely incredible. Now, Aoife and Blake are besties, their bond is so powerful. And during the pregnancy, the three of us were so close, living in the house together and trying to bring our baby into the world. We were having so much fun. If anything, I think that's what Aoife misses – that time together with Brian and me. But she's here all the time, taking Blake for a walk and visiting with us. The whole experience has brought us all closer than ever before.

Aoife cannot wait to have her name removed from Blake's birth certificate. We have every hope that by the end of 2023, both of Blake's fathers' names will be on her legal document and Aoife's name will be taken off. My child doesn't have a mother, but that's okay. She has two loving fathers, an incredible aunt, along with her many other aunts; she has uncles, cousins and a wonderful grandmother in my mum and grandfather in Brian's dad. There are so many different types of families now due to numerous circumstances, and the most important thing in all of those families is the unconditional love the child is raised with.

I've only been living in Ireland for the last three years, and a year of that was spent in lockdown, but look at everything that's happened in that time. I am so grateful and live every day of my life as if it was my last day on earth. I still have panic attacks now and again, waking up thinking I'm back in Armenia. I'm still scared. Brian would always say to me, 'You're never happy with what you have.' I am happy, but I will never stop working on my life. That said, since Blake was born, I am truly grateful for everything in my life. I look at her while she sleeps and just cry. Normally, I'm very strong but ever since she was born, I am so emotional. I can't believe I actually have the family I've always wanted.

One of the reasons why I want a sibling for Blake is because Brian and I aren't getting any younger and I want her to have someone beside her to grow old with so they have each other through it all. I have Nazik, and Brian has his six sisters. I want that for Blake. God knows if we'll be blessed with a second or third child or maybe it will never happen, but we do want to make it happen. It'll be another rollercoaster to get there but we're ready for it.

One thing I have learned since the birth of my daughter is that I never knew I could love someone this much. I would jump in front of a car for Blake. I never realised a love like this can hurt. I'm not going to lie and say I've become stronger or less selfish. I'm still loving life, I still do things for myself, but everything I do now is for Blake, for our future. I'm not a changed man, just my life is filled with more love now.

If you can take anything from my story it's that I'm living proof that anything is possible if you put your mind to it and work hard, if you remain positive and show kindness. Don't let anyone stop you from living the life you want. Be true to yourself and do what pleases you. If you want to watch a movie that received just one star, go for it. Who's to say you won't love that film? Don't be lazy – that's just wasting your potential. Get out and embrace life. And if something doesn't happen for you, if things don't go your way, it's not the end of the world. There's always something new waiting for you.

ACKNOWLEDGEMENTS

This book would not be possible without the help and support we have received not just these last few months but throughout our whole lives. First and foremost, our beloved family and friends, who we're enormously grateful for each and every day. Each and every one of you have made a huge impact on our lives and deserve your own mention, but before we each go into the individuals that have helped bring us to this point in our lives, we wish to thank the various people who helped bring this book to fruition. To the entire team at Gill Books, in particular Teresa Daly, who believed in us from day one and encouraged and supported us every step of the way; Meg Walker, who edited the book so diligently; Aoibheann Molumby, who shepherded the book through its final edits; our copyeditor Susan McKeever;

proofreader Kerri Ward; Sarah McCoy who designed the layout; and photographer Mark Nixon, who shot our beautiful family portrait for the cover. It takes a village, as they say, and we are thankful for all your hard work and care bringing this book to life. Now, we'd like to individually address the people in our lives who inspired the stories across these pages ...

BRIAN:

I wholeheartedly dedicate this book to my family, especially my mum, Rosie, who is no longer with us. Without your guidance and love, Mum, none of this would have been possible. All the sacrifices you made for me and the girls. I miss you every day.

To the light of my life, my daughter, Blake, you are my world. I feel like I've known you all my life. Your smile makes everything perfect.

To my six sisters – Michelle, Valerie, Tracey, Paula, Aoife and Tara – you have all shaped me into the person I am. I cherish each and every one of you. Our times together are so precious.

Now, Aoife, where do I even start with you? Thank you, thank you. You have changed my life and I shall be forever grateful.

To all my beautiful nieces and nephews – Chloe, Shannon, Sean, Leah, Sophie, Sadhbh, Rian, Harvey and baby Jesse – you guys are everything to us. In fact, I learned how to be a dad from each of you – especially you, Harvey, during the pandemic when Arthur and I lived back home. I will forever cherish those memories.

To my dad, Gerry, the quietest and most patient man ever, thank you for what you have done and still do for our family, especially after Mum's passing.

To my friends, who I consider my family. Thank you for picking me up when I couldn't get up, all the tears and the laughs. I adore you all.

To my husband and partner in crime, Arthur. Wow, what a journey we have been on, from our first meeting back in 2002 to where we are now. It's been one hell of a ride and we are just getting started. You are my calm in life. With you by my side, I know I'm going to be okay. You are my soulmate, my everything.

ARTHUR:

This book is dedicated to the loves of my life. Firstly, to the ultimate love of my life, our daughter Blake Maria Rose, who changed our lives *forever* the moment she entered our world, creating new and beautiful memories for us all from that day on. Blake, I can't wait to share every minute of my life with you.

Secondly, to my mum, Maria, aka Tati, thank you for everything you have done for Nazik and me. Without your encouragement and belief in me, I would have never made it here. You guided me in the right direction since day one. Only once in our lifetime did we have our 'ups and downs', but we came through, and what a beautiful journey we're having now. You are my *idol*.

To my sister, Nazik, who's always been there for me – my confidante, my best friend, and the person I can always rely on, thank you from the bottom of my heart. To my gorgeous nephew, Yohen, I love you so much and am so proud of the little man you have become. To my dad, Hakob, whom I miss every day, I wish you had the chance to see where we are now so I could make you proud.

Next, to my fantastic sister-in-law, Aoife, aka Effidy, who gave us the gift of our lifetime, *thank you*.

To those who helped my family and me and believed in me when I needed them, know that I appreciate each and every one of you. And to life itself for being a big challenge yet so, so beautiful and showing me that no matter what, life carries on, and it's what you make of it that matters.

And finally, to the man that I adore and am grateful for every day, Mr Brian Patrick Robert Dowling Gourounlian – *merci beaucoup, mon chéri. Je t'aime.*